Finding God in Everything

Spiritual Insights to Finding Everything in God

FINDING GOD IN EVERYTHING

Spiritual Insights to Finding Everything in God

Kuruvilla Pandikattu SJ

Jnana Deepa (JD)
2021

Finding God in Everything: Spiritual Insights to Finding Everything in God - Jointly published by Jnana Deepa (JD), Institute of Philosophy and Theology, Ramwadi, Nagar Road, Pune - 411014 and Indian Society for Promoting Christian Knowledge (ISPCK) Post Box 1585, Kashmere Gate, Madarsa Road, Delhi-110006

Online Order: http://ispck.org.in/book.php

ISBN: 978-81-947592-3-2

Sketches by: Shamil Joseph, Prabin RS RCJ

Laser typeset by

ISPCK, Post Box 1585, 1654, Madarsa Road, Kashmere Gate, Delhi-110006 • *Tel:* 23866323

e-mail: ashish@ispck.org.in • ella@ispck.org.in
website: www.ispck.org.in

Dedicated fondly to

Tina, Jerald, Jeremy and Jonathan

Tincy, Gingo and Noel

Contents

PART - III
FOSTERING CREATIVITY

PART - IV
DEEPENING SPIRITUAL PRACTICES

PART - V
NURTURING THE AESTHETIC

PART - VI

ENCOUNTERING THE DEPTH OF HUMAN VALUES

PART - VII

EMPOWERING THROUGH STORYING

PART - VIII

BEING ATTENTIVE TO THE SOCIETY

PART - IX
PROMOTING SOCIAL COMMITMENT

PART - X
DISCOVERING THE MEANING OF ME IN THE COSMOS

Foreword

God! Where do we find him? The simple answer is that he is to be found everywhere. In our hearts, in our neighbour and in the world! Thus, the living and loving God can be found in everyone and everything. It is surely a challenging task to find God in my enemies and the evil.

That is precisely what Prof Kuruvilla Pandikattu is trying to do in this creative book. He takes up some relevant issues for contemporary, creative spirituality, that is rooted in the world and in Christ. This book deals primarily with life as lived out in our daily lives. Then it tries to draw spiritual insight from the events of daily life, so that we can life up our lives, to embrace the world, fellow human beings and God. The approach that we take in this book is an inclusive and dialogical one, where we try to discern the divine in every aspect of the earthly life.

We believe that our spirituality emerges from the earthly, without in any way giving up the heavenly. We hold that true joy and happiness comc from thc simple pleasures of life. We hope that our fulfilment as human beings starts from our concrete experiences of joy, sadness, relationships and love.

Further, he goes on to find everything in God. That is another challenge. To find my friend, rival and my opponent in God. That implies that God is at work in him or her as much as he is at work in me. That challenges me to see the other in and through the eyes of God.

While congratulating Professor Pandikattu for bringing out this book, I wish that the readers will gain deep spiritual insights, which are truly rooted in the Christian experience of God's unconditional love for each one of us.

May we be enriched by reading this book and by tracing the Divine in every aspect of our lives!

Prof Stephane BAIK
Former Vice-Rector, Catholic University of Korea
President, Society of the Korean Society of Theology and Thought
Seoul, South Korea

Introduction

Who are we? How can we relate to others and thereby realise ourselves? What is the meaning of my life? Where do we find God? How do we relate to him? How does genuine spirituality enable me to become truly human, joyous and authentic?

These are some of the issues we take up in this book on contemporary, creative spirituality. This book invites us to find God in everything. Moreover, it invites us to find everything in God. It deals primarily with life as lived out in our daily lives in our interaction with things and God. Then it tries to draw spiritual insight from the events of daily life, so that we can live our lives, to embrace the world, fellow-human beings and God. The approach that we take in this book is an inclusive and dialogical one, where we try to discern the divine in every aspect of the earthly life.

So, we normally begin with a concrete experience, person, book or experiment. From that we go to explore the larger dimensions of life and study the deeper values inherent in it. So, we move from the material to the spiritual, from the mundane to the perfect, without in any way sacrificing the material or the mundane.

We believe that our spirituality emerges from the earthly, without in any way giving up the other-worldly. We hold that true joy and happiness comes from the simple pleasures of life. We hope that our fulfilment as human beings starts from our concrete experiences of joy, sadness, relationships and love.

In the first part of this book, we try ways and means of reaching happiness and healing. We want to show that our friends, relationships, memories and forgiving the harm others have done to us will enhance our well-being and bliss. The nextpart talks of the spiritual dimensions of our day to day life, which allows us to experience genuine joy. Meditations, mindfulness and other means of spiritual experiences are treated.

The third part invites us to foster creativity through art, silence and music, which form part of the melodies of our lives. Here we realise that our spiritual life has be rooted in the earthly and bodily aspects of our lives. This takes us to the next part, dealing with the spiritual practices leading to joy and optimism.

The abandonment that is critical to any spiritual life takes us to the next part, nurturing the aesthetic dimension of our lives. Art, dance, curiosity as well as reading and writing can make our life more authentic and empathetic. The sixth part helps us to explore some of deepest human values and tries to make the best of the encounters that we human beings are capable of encountering fellow human beings, the world and the whole of reality face to face. The next part describes the role of stories in healing, liberating and making our lives genuinely humane.

Part eight talks of our responsibility to the society and the need to pay attention to the joys and sorrows of the larger political, scientific and social dimension of our collective reality. The next part deals with our responsibility to make of this world a better one, recognising the larger (and at times, uncomfortable) truths of our social life.

Finally it talks about meaning and integrity within myself and in the larger world and cosmos we live in. It talks about the human need to be true to one's own self and to lead a modest and human life, so that we can truly feel at home with ourselves.

Thus, we want to show through this book that the God we seek (or conversely and even better, the God who seeks us continuously) is to be found in everyone and everything. He is present everywhere and traces of him can always be found in all things, if we are attentive enough.

That loving God is always present. From this experience, everything and everyone gets a different value. Then everyone has to be seen in God and everything has to be experienced in the Divine. So, we are called to find everyone and everything in God. That is grace! unconditional love and unqualified mercy.

Some of the articles are modified from my regular column in *Financial Chronicle* and I am grateful to them for the opportunity given to me for writing the article. I am immensely grateful to both Papal Seminary, Pune and Jnana Deepa (JD), Pune, for helping me birth this book. But for the academic environment and encouragement provided by my colleagues, this book would never have seen the light of day. I am eespecially grateful to the staff and students of Papal Seminary and particularly Rev Bhausaheb Sansare SJ and Rev Vincent Crasta SJ, Rector and Administrator. And to the staff and students of Jnana Deepa (JD) particularly Rev Selva Rathinam SJ, Rev Francis Gonsalves SJ and Rev Jose Thayil SJ, President and Registrar.

This book argues that the spiritual can be traced in all activities, earthly, mundane and secular. It assumes that we can only reach the spiritual in and through the secular, the ordinary experiences of normal human beings. All in all, this is a modest attempt to reflect on our contemporary lives and see the glimpse or traces of the Divine in our lives. It is an invitation to discern God's presence in everything and in everyone. It is a simple effort "to see God in everything." And further "to find everything in God" as St. Ignatius of Loyola would put it.

PART - I

Enabling Healing and Happiness

1

Owning Experiences, Not Things

The first part seeks to experience healing and happiness in our lives. We dwell on aspects of lives that need healing and on means which makes us genuinely happy. The first essay asks: Where can we find our joy? In things, persons or experience? A 20-year study conducted by Dr. Thomas Gilovich, a psychology professor at Cornell University, reached a powerful and straightforward conclusion: don't spend your money on things. The trouble with things is that the happiness they provide fades quickly.

Travis Bradberry (2009, the author of the bestseller *Emotional Intelligence 2.0*, point out three reasons for this. Firstly, we get used to new possessions. What once seemed novel and exciting quickly becomes the norm. Secondly, we keep raising the bar. New purchases of things lead to new expectations. As soon as we get used to a new possession, we look for an even better one. Thirdly, there are always better things to buy. Possessions, by their nature, foster comparisons. We buy a new car and are thrilled with it until a friend buys a better one – and there's always someone with a better one.

"One of the enemies of happiness is adaptation," Gilovich said. "We buy things to make us happy and we succeed. But only for a while. New things are exciting to us at first, but then we adapt to them" (Bradberry 2019).

This is the "paradox of possessions". Here we assume that "the happiness we get from buying something will last as long as the thing itself." Also it seems intuitive that investing in something we can see, hear and touch delivers the best value. It is definitely wrong.

Instead, Gilovich and others have found that "experiences – as fleeting as they may be – deliver more-lasting happiness than things."

Experiences become a part of our identity. We are not our possessions, but "we are the accumulation of everything we've seen, the things we've done and the places we've been," says Bradberry (2019).

"Our experiences are a bigger part of ourselves than our material goods," said Gilovich. "You can really like your material stuff. You can even think that part of your identity is connected to those things, but nonetheless they remain separate from you. In contrast, your experiences really are part of you. We are the sum total of our experiences" (Bradberry 2019).

Comparisons matter little. We don't compare experiences in the same way that we compare things, claims Bradberry. When people are asked if they'd rather have a high salary that was lower than that of their peers or a low salary that was higher than that of their peers, a lot of them aren't sure. But when they are asked the same question about the length of a vacation, most people choose a longer vacation almost always. It's hard to quantify the relative value of any two experiences, which makes them that much more enjoyable.

In this context, anticipation does matter. Gilovich also found that anticipation of an experience causes excitement and enjoyment, while anticipation of obtaining a possession causes impatience. Experiences are enjoyable from the very first moments of planning, all the way through to the memories you cherish forever.

Experiences are fleeting (which is a good thing). After we have brought something cool, it is usual that we get a bit bored and disappointed with it. It is called "buyer's remorse." And even if a purchase does meet your expectations, buyer's remorse can set in: "Sure, it's cool, but it probably wasn't worth the money" (Bradberry 2019). We don't do that with experiences. "The very fact that they last for only a short time is part of what makes us value them so much and that value tends to increase as time passes."

In short: The temporary happiness achieved by buying things only provides "puddles of pleasure." Such pleasure evaporates quickly and leaves us wanting more. But our experiences, though fleeting, have memories that linger more and provide us with more happiness and joy. Experiences enhance our identity. They make us happier than things.

Even more than things or experiences, I believe, it is persons who provide us with more enduring happiness. Our commitment to a person, both in good and bad times, provide us with happiness, even when things are not all in smooth. A long-term commitment to someone provides us with happiness beyond anything else.

Even more than things or experiences, I believe, it is persons who provide us with more enduring happiness.

2

Memory as Source of Healing

Healing is intimately connected with the healing of the past wounds, hurts and even trauma. Unless we reconcile ourselves with our own past, there cannot be genuine healing. This is true of both personal and societal healing. Pope Francis has something significant to tell us about our collective healing.

Pope Francis's visit to Armenia, June 24-26, 2016, is among the most breath-taking challenges he has faced. It defies both conventional wisdom and historical experience of the Armenian genocide. Also known as the Armenian Holocaust, it was the Ottoman government's systematic extermination of 1.5 million Armenians, mostly Ottoman citizens within the Ottoman Empire.

In this background Francis claims that the memory, even of holocausts, doesn't have to be dangerous, it can also be healing. He said it precisely in that corner of the planet "where competing memories of past wrongs are forever combustible," writes John L Allen, Editor, *Crux Magazine* (Allen Jr 2016).

Besides the death of 1.5 million people, at lower levels of magnitude, however, everyone in this neighbourhood seems to recall past wrongs, often fuelling suspicion, mistrust and the potential for new violence.

Precisely here comes Francis to deliver the opposite message – not only do you have a right to your memories, you're obligated to preserve them, even when they are tragic and painful.

"Not to forget them is not only right, it is a duty," he told the Armenians. "May they be a perennial warning lest the world fall back into the maelstrom of similar horrors!" At the same time, Francis insisted that the purpose of memory is not "to repeat the traumas of the past and certainly not to exact revenge for them, but rather to surpass them" (Allen Jr 2016).

So when he visited the Armenian genocide memorial, Francis wrote in the Book of Honour: "Memory must neither be watered down nor forgotten; it is the source of peace and of the future" (Allen Jr 2016). Naturally, the pope brings a spiritual equation to the argument: Add faith to memory and what you get is redemption: "Charity alone can heal memories and bind up past wounds," he said emphatically.

Later, he recalled several aspects of the "memory of a people". "As you ponder these things, you can clearly recognize God's presence," Francis said. "He has not abandoned you. Even in the face of tremendous adversity … He has remembered your faithfulness to the Gospel, the first-fruits of your faith and all those who testified, even at the price of their blood, that God's love is more precious than life itself" (Allen Jr 2016).

"It is good to recall with gratitude how the Christian faith became your people's life-breath and the heart of their historical memory," he said. Francis argued that the faith which memory supports expresses itself in mercy and concrete acts of love. Only such acts of merciful faith and memory can bring about healing, he added.

"We are called above all to build and rebuild paths of communion, tirelessly creating bridges of unity and working to overcome our divisions," Francis reminded the victims (Allen Jr 2016). Later, he elaborated his argument about memory. "Memory alone erases prejudices and makes us see that openness to our brothers and sisters can purify and elevate our own convictions," Francis said. "Memory, infused with love, becomes capable of setting out on new and unexpected paths, where designs of hatred become projects of reconciliation, where hope arises for a better future for everyone, where 'blessed are the peacemakers."

In all candour, Francis's version of the politics of memory may be a tough sell, where conflicts stories of holocaust and genocide makes common living very challenging. Still his optimistic message is that "new way of seeing the memories that so often sear the region – not only as a threat, but also a resource," writes Allen (2016).

Coming to our Indian situation, our spiritual depth and religious faith should enable us to accept the tremendous violence that we have done to others, implicitly and explicitly in the past. Both individually and collectively. At the same time, without belittling the violence, we need to tread, cautiously, the path of reconciliation and mercy. Without it, our future is uncertain!

> "Memory, infused with love, becomes capable of setting out on new and unexpected paths, where designs of hatred become projects of reconciliation, where hope arises for a better future for everyone, where 'blessed are the peacemakers'."

3

Effectiveness of Forgiveness

Connected with healing is the need for forgiveness? We dwell here with the forgiveness in our social or professional lives.

What is the role of forgiveness in workplaces? How does forgiveness affect our professional lives? Recent studies in workplaces supports the power of forgiveness to potentially improve well-being and productivity in professional settings. Researchers explored the role of forgiveness in reducing negative consequences in workplaces, writes Brook Deterline, CEO of Courageous Leadership (Deterline 2017).

Conflict among colleagues is inevitable and – left unheeded – associated with significant stress, health problems (both mental and physical) and reduced productivity. More than 200 employees working in office jobs in Washington, DC, or manufacturing jobs in the Midwest responded to questionnaires about their levels of forgiveness, productivity and well-being.

The first survey asked respondents to focus on a specific offence and how they believed it affected them. The second study looked at participants' general tendency to be forgiving and their general state of mind and work habits over the previous month.

In both cases, forgiveness was linked to increased productivity, decreased absenteeism and fewer mental and physical health problems, such as sadness and headaches. In the second study, these benefits were partly explained by reductions in interpersonal stress that went along with a forgiving disposition, elaborates Deterline (2017).

Moreover, the study found that a lack of forgiveness negatively affects the individuals involved and organizations. Holding on to negative feelings after a conflict may lead to disengagement at work, a lack of collaboration and aggressive behaviour. Carrying a grudge is also associated with increased stress and a host of negative emotions, including anger, hostility and vengeful rumination.

Since many people who have been in conflict need to continue to work together, forgiveness can be an effective coping tool and a way to repair relationships and restore trust – both of which are key to effective work cultures.

In 2012, Deterline and her team worked with employees at Google to build a more courageous culture, including the courage to forgive. They helped employees share times when they failed to act on their values at work, to admit they did not understand something, or to speak up when they thought they had a better idea. This was designed to remind everyone how easy it is to act outside of our values in stressful situations – to do something that might merit forgiveness.

Participants then practiced taking courageous action. They were helped to practice forgiveness by identifying current grudges and work on forgiving (not condoning) the behaviour. Participants also remembered and shared when others had forgiven them (Deterline 2017).

The program also showed positive impact. Participants reported a greater understanding of the power of stressful situations to negatively affect behaviour. They also reported feeling better and more connected afterward. One participant remarked: "I had a deepened sense of lightening inside, like letting go of heavy weights. I feel the forgiveness exercise for me was very powerful." Participants also took more social risks, like offering new ideas, admitting fears or concerns and asking for or offering help.

Research shows that this kind of forgiveness can even impact employees who aren't involved in the conflict. When people see others practicing forgiveness at work, it often fosters positive emotions that can improve decision-making, cognitive functioning and the quality of relationships, notes Deterline (2017).

"Resentment is like taking poison and waiting for the other person to die," she holds. If we are holding onto a grudge, we could be taking the poison and sharing it with our colleagues. Surely, forgiveness does not mean condoning or ignoring bad behaviour. We need to come up with policies and procedures for dealing quickly with serious transgressions in workplaces. We need to confront the offender firmly and gently.

However, we need to cultivate the courage to forgive, which alone can make the workplace a source of joy and creativity. For forgiveness, like Gandhi's non-violence, can emerge only from a position of strength.

> "Resentment is like taking poison and waiting for the other person to die!"

4

A Sense of Control Enhances Happiness

In this essay, we explore happiness and the need for control? How does technology help us to control our lives and contribute to our happiness?

So we ask: Are people who trust in technology happier than those who trust in God? A recent research suggests that religious people were happier and more satisfied with their lives, partly thanks to a greater sense of purpose and belonging. However, belief in God has declined over the past few decades in Western societies. What else, then, may people be turning to for security?

In recent study researchers Olga Stavrova, Daniel Ehlebracht and Detlef Fetchenhauer hypothesized that a belief in scientific and technological progress can also give this sense of purpose (Yip 2016) and happiness.

People who strongly believe in scientific-technological progress have faith that science and technology can help humanity build a better future. They're more likely to think that science and technology make our lives healthier, easier and more comfortable; create more opportunities for the next generation; and make the world better off, writes researcher Deborah Yip in *Greater Good Magazine* (Yip 2016).

The researchers first surveyed individuals in the Netherlands about this belief and about their religious faith, measured by how often they attended religious services and whether they identified themselves as religious and believed in God. They found that people who more strongly believed in scientific-technological progress or religion were more satisfied with their lives. Incredibly the link was significantly stronger among those who had faith.

When the researchers looked at the data from 72 countries, the researchers found that respondents with greater faith in science and technology were more satisfied with their lives in all but three countries; by comparison, being religious was positively associated with life satisfaction in only 28 countries – and linked to lower life satisfaction in five (Yip 2016).

What enables the belief in scientific-technological progress the power to be happier? Other researchers have recently proposed that a secular belief in human progress to reform the world, including faith in science and technology, gives us a sense of control. So Stavrova and her colleagues also asked participants about their sense of personal control: How much agency and influence did a sense of control give to their lives?

The answer was that people with greater trust in science and technology indeed tended to have a heightened sense of personal control – which was, in turn, linked to their higher life satisfaction. This suggests that "scientific understanding and use of technology may help us feel more in control of our environment and our future, buffering us against existential anxiety and leading to greater well-being. On the other hand, people who reported being more religious had a weaker sense of personal control."

Yip asks: What does this all mean for us? Is the study suggesting that a belief in science is better than a belief in religion? The study found that people who believe in science and technology are not less likely to be religious, suggesting that the two aren't necessarily incompatible. Both values can coexist and benefit us in different ways. Previous studies have found that people who are more religious tend to have a greater sense of "secondary control," the kind of strength we get from being able to accept and adjust to difficult circumstances.

In the end, "community may play an important role in how our beliefs support our well-being. In the international study, the research team found that the link between scientific-technological faith and life satisfaction was stronger in countries where this belief was popular" (Yip 2016).

So the author concludes that more than the specific beliefs we hold dearly, what is important is the fact that we have shared beliefs. Thus anything that helps us to control our lives – faith or science – can make our lives happier.

At the same time we need to develop a sense of critical appreciation over the control that we have through science and religion! Do they only give us a temporary sense of control? Can we also develop a sense of joy and happiness without this need to control our environment?

> We need to develop a sense of critical appreciation over the control that we have through science and religion!

5

The Number of Friends

Friends to contribute to our happiness and sense of well-being! How many close friends can we have? How does our inner circle shape us? How can we widen our circle of friends?

The University of Oxford anthropologist and psychologist, Robin Dunbar, became famous by his research on the size of animal's close companions gained some measure of fame more than 20 years ago. He discovered that each species of primate can manage to keep up a social bond with a certain number of other members of its own species. That number goes up as primates' brain size increases, from monkeys to apes.

Humans, Dunbar found, are capable of maintaining significantly more social ties than the size of our brains alone could explain, writes Julie Zauzmer in *The Washington Post* (Zausmer 2017). Dunbar proved that each human is surprisingly consistent in the number of social ties we can maintain: About five with intimate friends, 50 with good friends, 150 with friends and 1,500 with people we could recognize by name. These numbers, popularly known as "Dunbar's number," speaks of our close and extended social network (Zausmer 2017).

A related research finding on the place of God in our brains is interesting. Dunbar suggests that if "a person feels he or she has a close relationship with a spiritual figure, like God or the Virgin Mary, then that spiritual personage actually fills up one of those numbered spots, just like a human relationship would." This implies that one of our closest friends could be God.

And then Dunbar turned to figuring out why Dunbar's number is so high. Did humor help us manage it? Exercise? Storytelling? That riddle has been exciting Dunbar for many years. He seems to imply religion form part of the answer. "Most of these things we're looking at, you get in religion in one form or another," he said.

Zauzmer writes that Dunbar is just one of a recent waves of scientists who are interested in how religion came to be and how people have benefited from it. "For most of Western intellectual history since the Enlightenment, religion has been thought of as ignorant and strange and an aberration and something that gets in the way of reason," said Christian Smith, a sociologist at the University of Notre Dame who studies religion. "In the last 10 or 20 years on many fronts, there's been a change in thinking about religion, where a lot of neuroscientists have been saying religion is totally natural. It totally makes sense that we're religious. Religion has served a lot of important functions in developing societies" (Zausmer 2017).

But Smith thinks one can easily have faith in both God's truth and religion's role in human development. From a religious perspective we can claim: "God created humans as a very particular type of creature, with very particular brains and biology, just so that they would develop into the type of humans who would know God and believe in God" (Zausmer 2017).

Smith added that bringing God to these discussions do not discredit science, nor religion. He is certain: "They're not in conflict at all." To elaborate: "A lot of people assume, falsely, that science and religion are zero-sum games: that if science explains something, then religion must not be true. … If you were God and wanted to set up the world in a certain way, wouldn't you create humans with bigger brains and the ability to imagine?" (Zausmer 2017).

The large number of friends and companions we can embrace is definitely an asset. The more may not be always the merrier, here. More than building up our own personal relationships, these friends can help us to embrace the whole humanity and nature. Such an embrace of the whole is truly a religious experience.

A person can have a number of friends: About five with intimate friends, 50 with good friends, 150 with friends and 1,500 with people we could recognize by name.

6

Moving from Boredom to Happiness

How does boredom or activities contribute to our happiness? Can we be like Mary, doing nothing and still be deeply contended? This is the issue we discuss in this chapter.

Derek Beres the Los Angeles author of *Whole Motion: Training Your Brain and Body for Optimal Health* (Beres 2017) refers to a friend of his. He mentioned that he's looking forward to autonomous cars, as it will help lower the accident and fatality rates caused by distracted driving. Beres's initial response was true, with a caveat: what we gain on the roads we lose in general attention. Having yet another place to be distracted does not add to our mental and social health and happiness.

Little good comes from being distracted yet we seem incapable of focusing our attention. Among many qualities that suffer, recent research shows creativity takes a hit when you're constantly busy. Being able to switch between focus and daydreaming is an important skill that's reduced by insufferable busyness. As Stanford's Emma Seppälä writes: "The idea is to balance linear thinking – which requires intense focus – with creative thinking, which is borne out of idleness. Switching between the two modes seems to be the optimal way to do good, inventive work" (Beres 2017).

She is not the first to point this out. Neuroscientist Daniel Levitin (2015) made a similar plea in his 2014 book, *The Organized Mind*. Information overload keeps us mired in noise. In 2011, he writes, Americans consumed five times as much information as 25 years prior; outside of work we process roughly 100,000 words every day.

This saps us of not only willpower (of which we have a limited store) but creativity as well. He uses slightly different language than Seppälä – linear thinking is part of the central executive network, our brain's ability to focus, while creative thinking is part of our brain's default mode network. Levitin, himself a former music professional who engineered records by the Grateful Dead and Santana, writes:

Artists recontextualize reality and offer visions that were previously invisible. Creativity engages the brain's daydreaming mode directly and stimulates the free flow and association of ideas, forging links between concepts and neural modes that might not otherwise be made. Engaging creatively requires hitting the reset button, which means carving space in your day for lying around, meditating, or staring off into nothing (Beres 2017).

This is impossible when every free moment – at work, in a queue, at a red light – we're reaching for our phone. Our brain's attentional system becomes accustomed to constant stimulation; we grow antsy and irritable when you don't have that input. We become addicted to busyness.

And that's dangerous for quality of life. As Seppälä points out many of the world's greatest minds made important discoveries while not doing much at all. Nikola Tesla had an insight about rotating magnetic fields on a leisurely walk in Budapest; Albert Einstein liked to chill out and listen to Mozart on breaks from intense thinking sessions. Thus leisure, breaks and boredom are crucial for creativity.

Paying homage to boredom – a valuable tool in the age of overload – journalist Michael Harris (2015) writes in *The End of Absence* that we start to value unimportant and fleeting sensations instead of what matters most. He prescribes less in the course of a normal day. "Perhaps we now need to engineer scarcity in our communications, in our interactions and in the things we consume. Otherwise our lives become like a Morse code transmission that's lacking breaks – a swarm of noise blanketing the valuable data beneath" (Beres 2017).

Seppälä makes four suggestions to disconnect at a time where connection is always demanded of us:

1. Make a long walk – without your phone – a part of your daily routine.

2. Get out of your comfort zone.

3. Make more time for fun and games.

4. Alternate between doing focused work and activities that are less intellectually demanding.

That last one is also recommended by Cal Newport (2018), author of *Deep Work*. Newport is not on any social media and only checks email once a day, perhaps and even that time is strictly regimented. What seems to be lost in being "connected" is really irreplaceable time gained to focus on projects. Without that time, he says, you're in danger of rewiring your neural patterns for distraction.

If we spend our time in a state of frenetic shallowness and we *permanently* reduce our capacity to perform deep work. That is not a good sign for those who wish to perform creatively, which in reality is all of us. Research shows that the fear of missing out (FOMO) increases anxiety and takes a toll on your health in the long run. Of all the things to suffer, creative thinking is one of our greatest losses. Regardless of your vocation a flexible mindset openness to new ideas and approaches is invaluable. Losing it just to check on the latest tweet or post or an irrelevant selfie is an avoidable but sadly sanctioned tragedy.

Thus accepting our boredom leads to authenticity and creativity. It fosters depth and persistence in thinking. So break, leisure, boredom and pause are necessary ingredients for happiness.

> The idea is to balance linear thinking – which requires intense focus – with creative thinking, which is borne out of idleness. Switching between the two modes seems to be the optimal way to do good, inventive work!

7

Can I be Happier?

Once we have attained happiness, are we fully in it? Or do we want to more? The urge for more happiness can spoil our enjoyment, just like "the best (or better) is the enemy of the good."

'Love Island' is 2015 TV show, where a group of men and women participate in a series of tasks with a partner that they keep swapping till they meet the love of their life.

In this TV show the contestants have the opportunity to stick with their current partner or choose another member from the group, including any of the new arrivals. For relationship psychologist Dr Anjula Mutanda, the show is a microcosm of the seemingly infinite choice seemingly offered by society. The show offers "steady supply of good-looking people being poured into the show almost on a daily basis. It's similar to dating online where you are putting your best face forward, everyone's smiling and looking fabulous," she explains (Begum 2018).

Their now-infamous tagline "I'm happy but I could be happier" is the "epitome of this throwaway culture and the idea that the grass could always be greener." Dr Mutanda calls this excuse a 'dissatisfaction gap,' "when you live in a world where there's so much choice and when something has gone wrong in a relationship, there's a compulsion to be better off in a different situation" she says. "Instead of working on what you have, you're looking over your partner's shoulder constantly" (Begum 2018).

Dr Sheri Jacobson, counsellor at Harley Therapy, agrees that 'Love Island' plays "on our desire to be tempted, reflecting current attitudes that render relationships and people disposable." But she hopes that the participants and viewers recognise that love is not "trading in" but rather it is about "finding someone really good – good enough to be doing the work together" (Begum 2018).

But eternally swapping and seeking for new partners can be dangerous because though your choices may seem infinite, as Dr Mutanda puts it: "When will you know when you've found them?"

This insatiable search for novelty lies in the human nature, according to Dr Mutanda. "We are programmed to be novelty seekers and as humans we are excited by something new, whether that's a person, a shiny object or even a show," she says. The illusion of infinite choice can "stop you from being in the moment and working on what you've got," says Dr Mutanda. "Going from one person to another ends up in a misery cycle."

Dr Jacobson believes that the "I'm happy but I could be happier" is mantra true of both male and female. "Always seeking the possibility of better is problematic because it's the same as looking for another person to complete you and add meaning to your life. The best relationships happen when you're at ease and peace with each other and accept and love yourself," asserts Dr Jacobson (Begum 2018).

But this can only occur when you're emotionally mature and in tune with yourself, writes journalist Tahmina Begum in *HuffingtonPost*. Dr Mutanda adds that this tendency has nothing to do with age, as you can have an incredibly mature 25-year-old versus an immature 55 year old. "The biggest gift you can give yourself is knowing who you are. When you don't know who you are, you are chasing everything around and that's when you're not satisfied because you don't know what happiness means to you". But we need to realise that this excitement wears off and real life begins.

"The honeymoon period is a literal chemical high where you can't see any flaws and when this period is over, you start to see the differences," says Dr Mutanda. There is nothing wrong with seeing differences or having conflicts, but it's how you deal with the disagreements, that really shape our lives and our love.

To be constantly searching for the mirage of perfect and happier life itself may lead us to unhappiness. This is the paradox of love and happiness. We need to have wings that will give us more opportunities and possibilities. But without the roots (commitment, belongingness and security) to hold fast to, wings will never give us the sense of fulfilment. This reminds us of Shakespeare who said, "Striving to better, oft we mar what's well."

> "I'm happy but I could be happier" is the epitome of this throwaway culture and the idea that the grass could always be greener.

8

Happiness as By-Product

Finally, we become aware that happiness appears on our struggling and painful journey of living. It is not an end, but a by-product of our craving, longing and failing.

"Our happiness comes not as a goal, but as a by-product of engaging in honesty with ourselves," claims Susan David (2016), author of *Emotional Agility,* a leading psychologist at Harvard Medical School. She says that relentless positivity, which says "Be positive, be happy, have a great mood and everything will be fine," doesn't lead to happiness. Instead emotional honesty can enable us to be happy (Editors 2017).

What does it take internally in the way we deal with our thoughts, emotions and stories, to help us thrive in the world? Her finding is counter-intuitive: "Just be happy. What's wrong with you? Have a good attitude," does not help.

She elaborates in a conversation with *Heleo.com* entitled "Embrace Authenticity: How to Break Free from the Tyranny of Positivity": "I had my own experience with this when I was 15 years old. My father was diagnosed with terminal cancer and I had this group of people coming to me and saying, 'Just be positive. Everything will be okay.' It wasn't okay. My father was dying and then dead. I engaged in a relationship with this amazing teacher who instead of saying, 'Just be positive,' she showed up to me. She invited me to explore in a journal what I was going through. What did help was engaging with myself in a way that was honest" (Editors 2017).

One of her friends, who died of cancer speaks of "focus on being happy all the time as the tyranny of positivity." She adds: "By telling us to just be and think positive, it makes us feel culpable in our own death, that somehow we weren't positive enough. We couldn't think ourselves out of the situation. It stops me from being authentic with myself, with my experience and being able to be present with the people that I love."

Her conclusion is that people who focus on being happy actually, over time, become less happy. Our happiness comes not as a goal, but as a by-product of engaging in honesty with ourselves.

For this we need to reveal ourselves. Instead of trying to push our emotions aside or trying to put on a happy face instead, literally drop any struggle that you have within yourself by ending the battle. Not saying to yourself, "I'm unhappy, but I shouldn't be unhappy" (Editors 2017)

Really just open up to the fact that we have a full range of emotions. These emotions have helped us and evolved to enable us to position ourselves effectively in the world. "Our difficult emotions point to the things that we value." We can learn to step out of our emotions. It's important to recognize that our emotions contain data.

Instead of struggling with our emotions, it's important for us is to ask, "What is the function of this emotion? What is the value? What is this emotion trying to tell me?"

Here it is important to recognize that our emotions are data, not directions. Because I feel guilty, it doesn't mean I need to feel guilty. We can create space, the "stepping out" part. Her experience is that if we step out and get to know ourselves, if we slow down enough, figure out what is really going on, give ourselves space to complain, to write, it allows us to get unstuck. This enables us to be happy, not as goal, but as byproduct.

She refers to Viktor Frankl, the survivor of Nazi death camps, who says: "Between stimulus and response there is a space and in that space is our power to choose and it's in that choice that comes our growth and freedom" (Editors 2017). So often, we get hooked by our emotions. We treat them as fact, leaving no space between the stimulus and response. That precious little space enables us to be free, authentic and fulfilled!

Genuine happiness comes as we seek to make others happy. It cannot be bought or even sought. It emerges as we struggle with our commitment, without relationship and without labour. It appears when we work to reduce the pain of the other and alleviate the suffering around us. So, Eleanor Roosevelt is right: "Happiness is not a goal; it is a by-product."

> Genuine happiness cannot be bought or even sought. It emerges as we struggle with our commitment, without relationship and without labour.

PART - II

Fostering Joy Through Spiritual Experiences

9

Genuine Spiritual Life for Our Posterity

This part that deals with genuine joy attempts to find it in spiritual experiences. It is hoped that our spiritual longing and activities can further our authenticity and fulfilment. The first article shows that our search for spiritual life is not limited to ourselves, but includes also our children and larger family.

Beginning in the early 1970s, academicians began to acknowledge that religious belief is not against emotional wellbeing, challenging assumptions that was earlier social sciences. Later research moves beyond when experts believe that "church-goers and the devout tend to be less suicidal, more physically and mentally resilient, avoid at-risk behaviors and have stronger protective relationships buffering them from the vicissitudes of life."

Now, in an attempt to bridge research on spirituality with public awareness, Lisa Miller, professor and director of clinical psychology at Columbia University and director of the Spirituality Mind Body Institute, travels the country encouraging the parents "to nurture their innate spiritual abilities" for the sake of their kids. Religiously aware adolescents who feel connected to a higher power are 40 percent less likely to abuse substances, 60 percent less likely to battle depression and 80 percent less likely to engage in at-risk sexual behaviors," claims Betsy VanDenBerghe, a writer based in Salt Lake City, USA (VanDenBerghe 2016).

Miller finds scientifically plausible the notion that human beings, particularly teenagers and young adults, are "wired for transcendence and possess inborn spirituality" that must be used – or lost. While growing up, she herself benefitted from her mother's prayers and her father's quiet sharing of spiritual moments, like the time his deceased mother appeared to him in a dream and assured him she would always be his mother.

Calling spiritual connection a "buffer" not only against substance abuse, but also against "cortical thinness" of the brain associated with Alzheimer's and depression, Miller recommends that secular adults overcome their reluctance about religious practices so that their children avoid finding pseudo-transcendence through drugs, alcohol and sex. But ambivalence runs deep, she says and "doubtful parents, often wary of hypocrisy, tend to ignore children's spiritual-awakening experiences and questions" (VanDenBerghe 2016).

Miller's is relevant in our secular age, which is often ambivalent about religion. In this context, Miller's work represents a religious way of life for those wanting to opt into spiritual life. She attempts to "correct a skewed bell curve of spiritual IQ, driven down by a cultural discourse which can be pervasively clueless about the experiential nature of religious belief." It is sad that religious people are seen by many as clinging to outdated religious mores destined for extinction. And in the wings, a more radical anti-theist strain of New Atheism further polarize the dialogue with their mission to save naive children from superstitious indoctrination and pave the way for "enlightened" discourse, writes VanDenBerghe (2016).

VanDenBerghe shows that Miller's approach, however, mirrors that of the true sages of spiritual belief. Blaise Pascal, C.S. Lewis, William James and others understood that while conversion experiences involve the mind, they also require a great deal of the heart, soul and body. "Connecting spiritual dots, recognizing divine prompts and undergoing transcendent experiences take precedence over sheer empiricism, something secularists have a hard time understanding with their emphasis on proof," but all of which William James (2019) called essential to the *Varieties of Religious Experience*, in which, writes James, "There lie potential forms of consciousness entirely different" from our normal consciousness.

Teaching those forms of spiritual consciousness benefits not just our children, Miller observes, but a family's posterity at large. Spirituality passed from one generation to the next is 80 percent protective again depression. But when parents' spirituality combines with that of grandparents, an even greater buffer exists. Offering "spiritual treasure" to our posterity can become their greatest inheritance, writes VanDenBerghe (2016).

"Let them at least learn what this religion is which they are attacking before attacking it," Blaise Pascal (1972) wrote in his *Pensées*, explaining that God shows himself only to "those who genuinely seek him…with all their heart." Such a search changes our lives positively. It gives to our children and grandchildren something flexible and creative to hold on. It protects our posterity from self-inflicted harm and unavoidable depression!

God shows himself only to "those who genuinely seek him…with all their heart." Such a search changes our lives positively.

10

Matter, Mathematics and Mindfulness

Our search for God originates in our experience of this world. That experiences which opens to a reality larger than this world. Mathematics is the best example for such an experience. So in this section, we see how matter, mind and mathematics can invite us to experience a God beyond everything.

What is the probability for the existence of a supernatural God? In his 2016 book, *God? Very Probably: Five Rational Ways to Think about the Question of a God*, Robert H. Nelson (2016), Professor of Public Policy at the University at Maryland, examines this question. He looks at physics, the philosophy of human consciousness, evolutionary biology, mathematics, the history of religion and theology to show that the probability of God's existence may be quite high.

Physicist – and subsequent Nobel Prize winner – Eugene Wigner raised a fundamental question: Why did the natural world always obey laws of mathematics? In other words: Why do the laws of nature reflect the laws of mind?

How come the mathematical or conceptual laws discovered by mathematicians correspond to the laws of the real world? It may be noted that modern mathematics generally is formulated before any natural observations are made and many mathematical laws today have no known existing physical analogues (Nelson 2017).

Einstein's 1915 general theory of relativity, for example, was based on theoretical mathematics developed 50 years earlier by the great German mathematician Bernhard Riemann that did not have any known practical applications at the time of its intellectual creation.

Despite the many other enormous advances of modern physics after Einstein, little has changed in this regard. So Wigner wrote, "the enormous usefulness of mathematics in the natural sciences is something bordering on the mysterious and there is no rational explanation for it."

So writing in the newspaper, *Independent*, Nelson (2017) argues for the existence of a God to make the mathematical underpinnings of the universe comprehensible.

Similarly, in 2004 the great British mathematicial and Nobel laureate Roger Penrose put forward a vision of a universe composed of three independently existing worlds – mathematics, the material world and human consciousness. As Penrose acknowledged, it was a complete puzzle to him how the three interacted with one another outside the ability of any scientific or other conventionally rational model.

How can physical atoms and molecules, for example, create something that exists in a separate domain that has no physical existence: human consciousness?

It is a mystery that lies beyond science, claims Nelson (2017). This mystery is the same one that existed in the Greek worldview of Plato, who believed that abstract mathematical ideas first existed outside any physical reality. The material world that we experience as part of our human existence is an imperfect reflection of these prior formal ideals. These formal (mathematical) ideals point to God.

In fact, in 2015 the MIT physicist Max Tegmark (2015), argues in *Our Mathematical Universe* that mathematics is the fundamental world reality that drives the universe. So, mathematics is god-like.

The workings of human consciousness are similarly miraculous. Like the laws of mathematics, consciousness has no physical presence in the world; the images and thoughts in our consciousness have no measurable dimensions.

Yet, our nonphysical thoughts somehow mysteriously guide the actions of our physical human bodies. This is no more scientifically explicable than the mysterious ability of nonphysical mathematical constructions to determine the workings of a separate physical world.

Until recently, the scientifically unfathomable quality of human consciousness inhibited the very scholarly discussion of the subject. Since the 1970s, however, it has become a leading area of enquiry among philosophers (Nelson 2017).

So, the larger issue is reconciling the levels of material, mathematics and consciousness or mindfulness? How and why are these disparate entities so closely related? Should we not postulate a Divine to explain the necessary link between these three levels of our existence?

In other words, the necessary relationship between the physical world, logical concepts and conscious awareness demand a deeper explanation, which a deeper existence, the Divine, can provide. Does not the miraculous nature of our lives demand a miracle-enabler? That our physical, logical and conscious worlds converge is itself a miracle!

> "The enormous usefulness of mathematics in the natural sciences is something bordering on the mysterious and there is no rational explanation for it."

11

Enhancing Spirituality Biologically

From our study of mathematics, we come to biology. In this essay, we ask: How do we move to God from our physical or biological experiences? Do hormones deepen spirituality? Does medication make us better? The hormone oxytocin has been dubbed the "love hormone" for its role promoting social bonding, altruism and more. Now new research from Duke University suggests the hormone may also enhance spirituality and religious openness.

The new study reported a greater sense of spirituality shortly after taking oxytocin and a week later. Participants who took oxytocin also experienced more positive emotions during meditation, claimed lead author Patty Van Cappellen, a social psychologist at Duke Durham, North Carolina, USA, according to a report in DukeToday, authored by Alison Jones (Duke University 2016).

"Spirituality and meditation have each been linked to health and well-being in previous research," Van Cappellen said. "We were interested in understanding biological factors that may enhance those spiritual experiences." He added: "Oxytocin appears to be part of the way our bodies support spiritual beliefs."

Study participants were all male and the findings apply only to men, said Van Cappellen, associate director of the Interdisciplinary and

Behavioral Research Center at Duke's Social Science Research Institute. In general, oxytocin operates somewhat differently in men and women, the lead author added. Oxytocin's effects on women's spirituality still need to be investigated.

Oxytocin occurs naturally in our body. Produced by the hypothalamus, it acts as a hormone and as a neurotransmitter, affecting many regions of the brain. It is stimulated during sex, childbirth and breastfeeding. Recent research has highlighted oxytocin's possible role in promoting empathy, trust, social bonding and altruism.

To test how oxytocin might influence spirituality, researchers administered the hormone to one group and a placebo to another. Those who received oxytocin were more likely to say afterwards that spirituality was important in their lives and that life has meaning and purpose. This was true after considering whether the participant reported belonging to an organized religion or not.

Participants who received oxytocin were also more inclined to view themselves as interconnected with other people and living things, giving higher ratings to statements such as "All life is interconnected" and "There is a higher plane of consciousness or spirituality that binds all people" (Duke University 2016). It may be noted that spirituality may be understood in very different levels, by different cultures, religions and worldviews. Still there are clear commonalities in the way we understand the spiritual depth and spiritual way of life.

The experimental study subjected also participated in a guided meditation. Those who received oxytocin reported experiencing more positive emotions during meditation, including awe, gratitude, hope, inspiration, interest, love and serenity, writes Jones (Duke University 2016).

Oxytocin did not affect all participants equally, though. Its effect on spirituality was stronger among people with a variant of the CD38 gene, a gene that regulates the release of oxytocin from hypothalamic neurons in the brain. This implies that spiritual performance is affected by chemical, biological and genetic alterations.

Van Cappellen cautioned that the findings should not be over-generalized. First of all, there are many definitions of spirituality, she noted. "Spirituality is complex and affected by many factors," Van Cappellen said. "However, oxytocin does seem to affect how we perceive the world and what we believe" (Duke University 2016).

Spirituality is a way of relating to the larger world, including God and maybe enhanced by biological and chemical elements. That does not imply that spirituality may be reduced to its biological and chemical components. It does imply that spirituality, our way of making sense of life, is deeply embedded in our physical and chemical composition. Every attempt at enhancing or deepening such a spirituality must be appreciated.

Further the study indicates that spiritualty is intricately connected to love, altruism and a sense of bondedness of interconnectedness. Biological factors like medicine and hormones may enhance our spiritual life. Thus, to be spiritual implies that we are deeply aware of and open to others sympathetically. We are biologically wired for it.

Biological factors like medicine and hormones may enhance our spiritual life. Thus, to be spiritual imply that we are deeply aware of and open to others sympathetically. We are biologically wired for it.

12

Can Drugs Enhance Our Spiritual Experience?

If biology can enhance our spiritual journey, what about hormones and drugs? Can controlled intake of drugs enhance religious experience. Can we compare the functioning of such drugs with other religious practices like prayer and meditation?

An ongoing study by scientist at Johns Hopkins University in Baltimore studies the effects of drugs on religious experience. The experiment aims to assess whether a transcendental experience alters the participants' religious thinking (Carey 2019).

The study enlisted two dozen religious leaders from a wide range of denominations, to participate in a study where they were given two powerful doses of psilocybin, the active ingredient in magic mushrooms, a psychedelic drug that causes hallucination and expands consciousness.

Dr. William Richards, a psychologist at Johns Hopkins University in Baltimore, Maryland who is involved in the work, said: "With psilocybin these profound mystical experiences are quite common" (Carey 2019).

The experiment, which is currently underway, aims to assess whether a transcendental experience makes the leaders more effective and confident in their work and how it alters their religious thinking, reports Hannah Devlin, Science correspondent, The Guardian.

It is true that organised religions do not approve of the use of illicit substances. After preliminary screening, including medical and psychological tests, the participants were given two powerful doses of psilocybin in two sessions, one month apart.

The sessions were conducted in the presence of two "guides." The participants were given the drug and then spend time lying on a couch, wearing eyeshades and listening to religious music on headphones to augment their inward spiritual journey.

"Their instruction is to go within and collect experiences," Richards said. "So far everyone incredibly values their experience. No one has been confused or upset or regrets doing it."

A full analysis of the outcomes will take place after a one-year follow-up with the participants, whose identities are being kept anonymous. "It is too early to talk about results, but generally people seem to be getting a deeper appreciation of their own religious heritage," he said. "They discover they really believe this stuff they're talking about."

There is also a suggestion that after their psychedelic journey, the leaders' notions of religion shifted away from the sectarian towards something more universal. "They get a greater appreciation for other world religions. Other ways up the mountain, if you will," said Richards (Carey 2019).

"In these transcendental states of consciousness, people seem to get to levels of consciousness that seem universal," he added. "So a good rabbi can encounter the Buddha within him."

The notion that such drugs can bring about mystical experiences is not new and was previously studied in a famous Harvard study known as the "Good Friday experiment". The study involved a group of young religious students being given psilocybin, which altered their experience of prayer and religious celebrations. The latest work is thought to be the first involving religious leaders from different faiths.

The John Hopkins team are one of several research groups around the world making the case for using psychedelic drugs, such as psilocybin, LSD and MDMA, in psychiatry and possibly in religion. Psilocybin has been shown to be remarkably effective at lifting acute anxiety in cancer patients at the end of life, while other current trials are looking at the use of psychoactive drugs in treating conditions ranging from post-traumatic stress disorder to severe depression and alcoholism.

Is it legitimate to use such drugs to enhance religious experiences? While many, including this writer, have reservations, Richards is enthusiastic about the broader, non-medical, uses of psychedelic drugs. "My wild fantasy is that, probably sometime after I'm long dead, these drugs are used" in spiritual training" (Carey 2019). There is no harm giving it a try, provided it is properly monitored. We can be critically and carefully open to it!

> After their psychedelic journey, the leaders' notions of religion shifted away from the sectarian towards something more universal. "They get a greater appreciation for other world religions. Other ways up the mountain, if you will,"

13

Negative Spirituality

In our search for spirituality, we also need to be aware that sometimes spirituality can have negative consequences. Spirituality itself, unfortunately, can become dehumanising. We need to be warned of it.

Can spirituality lead to negative consequences? Can we at least sometimes describe some forms of spirituality as negative? Negative spiritual beliefs are associated with more pain and worse physical, mental health, a recent scientific study has found. Individuals who blame God or karma for their poor health have more pain and worse physical and mental health, according to the study from University of Missouri, USA (University of Missouri 2015).Targeted interventions to counteract negative spiritual beliefs could help some individuals decrease pain and improve their overall health, the researchers said.

"In general, the more religious or spiritual you are, the healthier you are, which makes sense," said Brick Johnstone, a neuropsychologist and professor of health psychology in the MU School of Health Professions. "But for some individuals, even if they have even the smallest degree of negative spirituality – basically, when individuals believe they're ill because they've done something wrong and God is punishing them – their health is worse."

Johnstone and his colleagues studied nearly 200 individuals to find out how their spiritual beliefs affected their health outcomes. Individuals in the study had a range of health conditions, such as cancer, traumatic brain injury or chronic pain and others were healthy. The researchers divided the individuals into two groups: a negative spirituality group that consisted of those who reported feeling abandoned or punished by a higher power and a no negative spirituality group that consisted of people who didn't feel abandoned or punished by a higher power. Participants answered questions about their emotional and physical health, including physical pain.

Those in the negative spirituality group reported significantly worse pain as well as worse physical and mental health while those with positive spirituality reported better mental health. However, even if individuals reported positive spiritual beliefs, having any degree of negative spiritual belief contributed to poorer health outcomes, the researchers found, as reported in *Technology.org* (University of Missouri 2015).

"Previous research has shown that about 10 per cent of people have negative spiritual beliefs; for example, believing that if they don't do something right, God won't love them," Johnstone said. "That's a negative aspect of religion when people believe, 'God is not supportive of me. What kind of hope do I have?' However, when people firmly believe God loves and forgives them despite their shortcomings, they had significantly better mental health" (University of Missouri 2015).

Individuals with negative spiritual beliefs tend to be participating in religious practices less frequently and having lower levels of positive spirituality and forgiveness. "Interventions that help combat negative spiritual beliefs and promote positive spiritual beliefs could help some individuals improve their pain and their mental health," Johnstone maintained (University of Missouri 2015).

Thus, more important than whether we believe in God are the two questions: Does my spirituality lead me to love God more? Does it lead to accepting others more lovingly and intimately?

Belief in God makes it easier to have genuine and liberative spirituality. Unfortunately, that need not always be the case. We can have firm faith in God which leads to negative and oppressive spirituality. In other words, even the most sacred object of religion and spirituality, namely, God can also be debilitating and enslaving.

Faith in God, the creator of the whole universe is a basic affirmation that the whole creation is God. Such a faith necessarily helps us to see the world as good and joyful, in spite of the evident evil and violence present in this world. Further, faith in God necessarily leads us to experience Him in our brothers and sisters, especially the vulnerable and underprivileged.

If our faith in God of spiritualty does not necessarily lead to a liberating God and to liberating fellow human beings, our faith is suspect. Such faith has tremendous negative and oppressive consequences.

So the most fundamental question a human being faces is: How does my encounter with God deepen my commitment to other human beings and the larger world? How does my spiritual life help me to embrace the other with joy, love and acceptance?

> If our faith in God of spiritualty does not necessarily lead to a liberative God and to liberating fellow human beings, our faith is suspect. Such a faith has tremendous negative and oppressive consequences.

14

Attaining Happiness by Defeating the Causes of Unhappiness

Our ancient spiritual or monastic traditions have something to contribute to our contemporary search for well-being and happiness.

What is the relevance of the ancient monastic life for today? How do spiritual realities enhance our daily living? *Finding Happiness: Monastic Steps for a Fulfilling Life* written by Christopher Jamison (2008) is an extremely useful book in attaining human fulfilment and happiness. It is Jamison's conviction that the monastic rules and writings have much to offer contemporary people as they search for fulfilment in life.

The Preface of the book states the writer's starting point succinctly: "The simple idea running through the whole book is that happiness comes to us indirectly as the fruit of defeating the causes of our unhappiness." The core of his work is then an analysis of the Eight Thoughts, which arise spontaneously but tend, if acted upon, to lead us away from all that makes for true human happiness. These thoughts were first categorised by Cassian, a fourth-century monk, writes Paul Nicholson, editor of the spirituality review, *The Way* (Nicholson 2008).

Pope Gregory the Great, two hundred years later, re-formulated the eight thoughts as the more familiar seven deadly sins, but two important elements were lost in this transformation. First, the Thoughts are not in themselves sinful. They draw us away from happiness and thus should be resisted, but there is nothing sinful about them. Second, Gregory omitted one, *acedia*, from Cassian's list. According to Jamison, *acedia* is a key concept if we want to understand the spiritual state of much of the world today.

For *acedia* is the inclination "to neglect spiritual realities, letting the cares, concerns and distractions of the everyday world fill my every waking moment" (Nicholson 2008). It can only be overcome by the kind of reflective self-awareness that our culture often regards as a waste of time. But without such reflection, we shall easily fall prey to the other Thoughts (like gluttony, lust, greed, anger, sadness, vanity and pride). By contrast sustained awareness of what is going on within us helps us to resist the pressure of the Thoughts and allows us to practice instead the corresponding virtues leading to genuine happiness, writes Nicholson.

This framework offers Jamison a way of commenting on many of the ills of contemporary society. Along the way he discovers many more similarities than might have been expected between the struggles faced by his own brothers trying to grow as good monks and those of hard-working family members attempting to live with integrity. The mental discipline underlying chastity, for instance, is not so different in those practising the vows of celibacy and married couples. Likewise, monks can be as tempted to acquire the latest electronic gadget as any teenager!

Jamison is suspicious of allowing ourselves to be guided by feelings in reaching important decisions. One chapter contrasts the experiences of feeling, knowing and doing good and of these feeling is very much the poor relation. He recognizes the need to sift through feelings and that some are more to be trusted than others. Overall perhaps Jamison has a greater confidence that understanding one's thought processes will be enough to enable one to do the good thing.

He passionately believes that we can achieve happiness by defeating the causes of unhappiness. So he deals mostly with the negative thoughts that impede happiness, although he speaks briefly of the eight contrasting Virtues (moderation to replace gluttony; chaste love instead of lust;

generosity overcoming greed; gentleness not anger; gladness rather than sadness; spiritual awareness banishing *acedia*; magnanimity supplanting vanity; and pride yielding to humility) (Nicholson 2008).

This book is a universally accessible guide to ways in which the monastic wisdom of the early Middle Ages is still relevant to contemporary persons, who want to understand what happiness really is and how it can be attained. Despite the tremendous technological growth and achievements, the human search for happiness remains the same. Also the means to find it remains constant. Thus we can best attain happiness by defeating the causes of unhappiness.

Despite the tremendous technological growth and achievements, the human search for happiness remains the same. Also the means to find it remains constant.

15

Joy as Being 'in the Flow'

Finally, we end this part by focussing on joy and spiritual life as being "in the flow." By swimming along with the current and by dancing rhythmically with the larger flow of life! Spirituality has been making an interesting comeback in recent years. Recently the trend has been not to focus too much on one's own initiatives to be spiritual. Rather, the idea is gaining ground than giving up control to some higher power/consciousness/energy, whatever that may be. In other words, being "in the flow."

But what's really fascinating about this idea is that it's not actually specific to spirituality: many people talk of feeling, under the right conditions, like they're in the flow, as if something greater has taken over and they're simply letting it happen. Writers, artists, musicians, designers, athletes and many others have experienced this state of flow, or being in the zone, writes Alice G. Walton in *Forbes* (Walton 2017).

She discusses the views of Ben Michaelis, PhD, a clinical psychologist and author of *Your Next Big Thing* (Michaelis 2013) makes a couple of points about what's likely going on when we get out of our own way and into the flow. The first comes from looking at the other end of the spectrum – when we are stressed, which might be considered the polar opposite of "flow." He points out that at these times, our thinking starts to suffer, sometimes in significant and bizarre ways. We tend to look for patterns where there are none and draw conclusions that do not exist (Walton 2017).

"A lot of research looks at what happens when you're stressed," he says. When we try to control things when we are tense, "we end up looking for patterns where they don't exist," says Michaelis (Walton 2017).

The other point he makes is that we are a species who, when we're young, are helpless and rely on other people to survive – doing so is built-in and it feels really good. This may be part of why we surrender (to anything outside ourselves – a caregiver, a greater power, etc.) feels secure. "We're an altricial species," needing much care and attention, says Michaelis. "We're wired for this, we're pretty much useless at birth. We must give up control to other people, or we die. So, in fact, we're wired to give up control – to trust others to have more knowledge than us." So again, there is something intrinsic about relinquishing control, that is not only a necessity but actually kind of delightful and stress-relieving.

Michaelis makes it look brilliant. He says that same delight in letting go also exists when we are witnessing great art unfold. When we can really surrender ourselves in the unfolding of a painting, poem, or music, we experience a type of abandonment or bliss. "It's like television writing," he says. "It's so good these days that you can relax into it and even give some leeway when an episode isn't so good – you know it'll be better down the line. It's like, 'Ok, I can relax'." It is that uncanny secure feeling of relaxing into the aptitude of another (Walton 2017).

Thus being 'in the flow,' is our natural way of developing and growing. Without any pretensions of the ego or others' expectations, we are given the possibilities to develop ourselves. In this process, on its own, we become closer to ourselves. In this process, we can work hard and relax; we can both struggle and enjoy; we can both let go of ourselves and be the master of ourselves!

This is true, not only of psychological phenomena. At the biological or physical level too, when we are at ease, when our bodies are relaxed, when we feel comfortable with our own physical bodies when we are "in the flow" we can achieve great things, without struggling. That is the spirituality of letting ourselves go and in the process, paradoxically, we fulfil ourselves! Thus we flow with the rest of the universe and the universe flows through our bodies! Rhythmically. That is true joy!

At the biological or physical level too, when we are at ease, when our bodies are relaxed when we feel comfortable with our own physical bodies when we are "in the flow" we can achieve great things, without struggling.

PART - III

Fostering Creativity

16

The Music of the Brain

In the last part we explored the possibility of fostering joy. In this part we explore the possibility of fostering creativity. For joy and creativity are closely tied. One of the unique features of human beings is creativity, that sets us apart from other creatures: creativity in art, language and culture.

Music is really one of the most creative aspects of human life. We shall see how music can enhance the brain functioning of the brain. The field of music and neuroscience is greatly expanding and is indicating many beneficial ways music can engage and change the brain. Let's discuss how music affects the brain and mood by engaging emotion, memory, learning and neuroplasticity and attention. In looking at the many ways that music engages the brain, we can begin to understand how creating a consistent musical program can target and enhance certain brain functions, writes, Barry Goldstein in *Conscious Life Style Magazine* (Goldstein 2016).

The four ways we can enhance the brain function through music are:

1. Playing an Instrument: Musical improvisation, which is a spontaneous creative idea, is a perfect example of how music affects both sides of the brain. Our technical skills are utilized to play the instrument and affect the left side of the brain, while the new creative ideas or improvisation flowing through us affect the right side. In addition, we are tapping into the power of our hearts by embedding the music with our emotion. On a spiritual level, when I improvise, I always feel like the ideas are flowing through me in collaboration and connection with a larger field and something outside myself. If you want to influence both your brain and heart with music, improvise! This practice is not limited to just musicians; I have seen many friends write their own lyrics to songs on karaoke night!

This skill of improvising is a powerful way music can affect your brain and mood. It can also be applied in different areas of our lives to find creative solutions and improve cognitive abilities and spontaneous thought, which in turn can assist with the challenges we face in our daily lives.

2. Singing even badly: In addition to singing having beneficial effects for our heart, it also affects our brain as well. Keep in mind that it is about the act of singing itself, not how well you sing! Some studies have demonstrated that singing (even bad singing!) provides emotional, social and cognitive benefits. In addition, music can affect our mood and can be used to improve speech function and decrease stress, anxiety and depression.

3. Chanting to Peace: For thousands of years, chanting as a form of music has been used as a vehicle to form a deeper spiritual connection in the brain and affect our mood. This is especially true of the sound Om, which is said to contain every sound in the universe within it (Goldstein 2016).

As we chant Om, for instance, we can release mind chatter through music and our focus shifts to a deeper spiritual connection. But chanting also benefits people's physical body as well as their spiritual one!

A pioneering study revealed that chanting the word om could engage the area of the brain that is associated with calmness and a sense of inner peace. Functional MRIs were used to scan the brain while people chanted different sounds and syllables, including Om. While chanting random sound showed no benefit, chanting om activated the area of the brain associated with a sense of peacefulness.

4. Drumming Collaboratively: Research indicates that specific musical beats can affect our mood by inducing different brain wave frequencies and can induce a deeply relaxed state. Other studies show that participation in group drumming led to significant improvements in many aspects of social-emotional behaviour. The potential of the benefits of drumming on the brain is leading to some amazing collaborations. Mickey Hart, former drummer of the Grateful Dead, paired with neuroscientist Dr. Adam Gazzaley in hopes of gaining a deeper understanding of how music directly affects different brain wave states and how it may help specific brain conditions. Dr. Gazzaley measured Hart's brain wave activity as he played at concerts. Hart led a drum circle of over a thousand people (Goldstein 2016).

It demonstrated the natural power of group rhythmic entrainment and their findings supported recent studies that indicated how playing a musical instrument can strengthen and exercise the ageing brain, writes Goldstein.

> Research indicates that specific musical beats can affect our mood by inducing different brain wave frequencies and can induce a deeply relaxed state. Other studies show that participation in group drumming led to significant improvements in many aspects of social-emotional behaviour.

17

Stoking Creativity

After looking at creativity and brain function, we see here how creativity can be enhanced in workplaces. There is an effective formula for unlocking employees' creative potential, according to new research from the McCombs School of Business at The University of Texas, Austin, USA and the Gies College of Business at the University of Illinois at Urbana-Champaign, USA. Employers should incentivize workers to produce an abundance of ideas – even mediocre ones – and then have them step away from the project for an "incubation period" (University of Texas at Austin 2019).

The researchers found that people who were rewarded simply for churning out ideas, whether good or bad, ultimately ended up producing more creative ideas than people who did not receive pay incentives or those whose pay incentives were based on the quality of their ideas instead of the quantity, reports *Daily Science*. All the study participants stepped away from the initial task for a time and returned to it later.

"Creativity is not instantaneous, but if incentives promote enough ideas as seeds for thought, creativity eventually emerges," said Steven Kachelmeier, the Randal B. McDonald Chair in Accounting at Texas McCombs and co-author of the study.

It has been well established in the academic literature that creative performance is enhanced by an incubation period, but this research looked at a new question: What happens when you add incentives for idea generation to the equation?

Kachelmeier and co-authors, Laura Wang and Michael Williamson, of the University of Illinois, conducted two experiments. In the first, they asked study participants to create rebus puzzles – riddles where words, phrases or sayings are represented using a combination of images and letters.

Some participants were offered pay based on the number of ideas they generated, some only for ideas that met a standard for creativity and others a fixed wage of $25, regardless of the quantity or quality of their puzzle ideas.

Initially, none of the incentivized groups outperformed the fixed-wage group in measures of creativity, as judged by an independent panel. Creativity incentives, it would seem, do not work instantly. But in a subsequent return to the creativity task 10 days later, those who had originally been paid to come up with as many ideas as they could had "a distinct creativity advantage," outperforming the other groups in both the quantity and quality of ideas, Kachelmeier said (University of Texas at Austin 2019).

Having an incubation period after participants put their minds to work was key to their success, the researchers said. Combining mass idea generation with a rest period results in much more creative productivity than when either of the two strategies is used in isolation.

How much time is needed? That is the question the researchers tackled in a second experiment, paying half the participants a fixed amount and half for the number of ideas they produced. As before, the pay-for-quantity participants yielded more, but not better, initial ideas than the fixed-pay group.

But after researchers led participants on a quiet, 20-minute walk around the campus, the pay-for-quantity group once again produced more and better puzzles, reports *ScienceDaily*.

"You need to rest, take a break and detach yourself – even if that detachment is just 20 minutes," Kachelmeier said. "The recipe for creativity is to try and get frustrated because it's not going to happen. Relax, sit back and then it happens" (University of Texas at Austin 2019).

Thus creativity is fostered by an incubation period and by monetary incentives. Getting frustrated, sitting back and trying again yields better insight. Economic benefit enhances creativity. Can we collectively create ideas and insights that benefit the whole humanity? Some remuneration will not damage it. But we cannot allow ourselves to be motivated only by economics.

Economic benefit enhances creativity. Can we collectively create ideas and insights that benefits the whole humanity? Some remuneration will not damage it. But we cannot allow ourselves to be motivated only by economics.

18

Creativity and Criticism

In this section we link creativity and criticism, especially in the workplaces. How can we empower someone who is not up to the mark without being overtly negative? How can we foster his or her self-image and creativity?

Though most firms today embrace a culture of criticism, when supervisors and peers dispense negative feedback it can stunt the creative process, according to a new study. In order to inspire the team creatively, we need to be more attentive to the employees' feelings and then deliver negative feedback respectfully. When supervisors or peers dispense negative feedback it can stunt the creative process, according to a new study co-authored by Yeun Joon Kim, a PhD scholar at the University of Toronto's Rotman School of Management (University of Toronto 2019).

Kim, who worked as a software engineer for Samsung before pursuing his graduate studies, is familiar with having his creative work scrutinized and criticised even mercilessly. "I personally hate hearing negative feedback – as most people do – and I wondered if it really improved my performance, particularly when it came to completing creative tasks," says Kim, who will join the Cambridge Judge Business School as an assistant professor, reports *ScienceDaily* (University of Toronto 2019).

This is an issue that many other researchers also are curious about. The literature has been mixed when it comes to determining whether criticism inspires or inhibits creative thinking. In this new investigation,

Kim and his co-author Junha Kim, a PhD student at Ohio State University, observed – through a field experiment and a lab experiment – and reported on how receiving negative feedback might impact the creativity of feedback recipients.

In both studies, Kim found that negative feedback can help or hinder creativity. What is most important is where the criticism comes from.

When creative professionals or participants received criticism from a boss or a peer, they tended to be less creative in their subsequent work. Interestingly, if an individual received negative feedback from an employee of lower rank, they became more creative. Some aspects of these findings seem intuitive, according to Kim.

"It makes sense that employees might feel threatened by criticism from their managers," says Kim. Supervisors have a lot of influence in deciding promotions or pay raises. So negative feedback from a boss might trigger career anxieties."

We can also understand how feedback from a co-worker might also be received as threatening. We often compete with our peers for the same promotions and opportunities. When we feel that pressure from above or from our peers, we tend to fixate on the stressful aspects of it and end up being less creative in our future work, says Kim (University of Toronto 2019).

What Kim found most surprising was how criticism proved to be beneficial for supervisors when the negative feedback came from their followers or employees, they are responsible for. "It's a bit counterintuitive because we tend to believe we shouldn't criticize the boss," says Kim. "most supervisors are willing to receive negative feedback and learn from it. It's not that they enjoy criticism – rather, they are in a natural power position and can cope with the discomfort of negative feedback better."

The key takeaways: bosses and coworkers need to be more careful when they offer negative feedback to someone they manage or to their peers.

And feedback recipients need to worry less when it comes to receiving criticism, says Kim (University of Toronto 2019).

"The tough part of being a manager is pointing out a follower's poor performance or weak points. But it is a necessary part of the job," says Kim. "If you are a supervisor, just be aware that your negative feedback can hurt your followers' creativity. Followers tend to receive negative feedback personally. Therefore, keep your feedback specific to tasks. Explain how the point you're discussing relates to only their task behaviour, not to aspects of the person."

And, in general, be kind and attentive. "Don't criticize recklessly. Anyone who wants to offer negative feedback on the job should do so – discreetly and sensitively," he adds. Criticism helps if done affirmatively, firmly and gently. If it is done out of love! For the sake of the common good.

> Criticism helps, if done affirmatively, firmly and gently. If it is done out of love! For the sake of the common good.

19

Art before Commerce

Creativity is part of our artistic dimension. Today both have become part of our commercial ventures. Can we save art from commerce? Human beings from being merchandise? In this connection a comic strip can help us.

The comic strip "Calvin and Hobbes," has become a classic. This timeless comic strip debuted in November of 1985 and came to an end in 1995.

Commonly cited as "the last great newspaper comic," Calvin and Hobbes have evinced broad and enduring popularity, influence and academic interest. Calvin and Hobbes follow the humorous antics of Calvin, a precocious, mischievous and adventurous six-year-old boy and Hobbes, his sardonic stuffed tiger (Dixit 2016). The pair is named after John Calvin, a 16th-century French theologian and Thomas Hobbes, a 17th-century English political philosopher. Set in the contemporary, suburban America, the strip depicts Calvin's frequent flights of fancy and his friendship with Hobbes ("Calvin and Hobbes – Art Before Commerce" 2016).

It further examines Calvin's relationships with family and classmates, especially the love/hate relationship between him and his classmate. Hobbes' dual nature is a defining motif for the strip: to Calvin, Hobbes is a live anthropomorphic tiger; all the other characters see Hobbes as an inanimate stuffed toy. Though the series does not mention specific political figures or current events, it does explore broad issues like environmentalism, public education, philosophical quandaries and the flaws of opinion polls

It remains meaningful and enjoyable whether you are 6 or 16 or 30. It is rare to meet someone who does not like Calvin and Hobbes. And new generations keep discovering the imaginative world of a mischievous six-year-old and his stuffed tiger with joy.

Its reclusive creator Bill Watterson has never given in to insistent demands of licensing the strip or its characters for merchandising or movies or video games or any other form. He explained his reasons in the introduction to the 1995 The Calvin and Hobbes Tenth Anniversary Book, writes Shubhra Dixit *Scroll.in* on May 25, 2016 (Dixit 2016).

Besides cheapening the original, he wrote, "The world of a comic strip ought to be a special place with its own logic and life, I don't want some animation studio giving Hobbes an actor's voice and I don't want some greeting card company using Calvin to wish people a happy anniversary and I don't want the issue of Hobbes' reality settled by a doll manufacturer. When everything fun and magical is turned into something for sale, the strip's world is diminished. Calvin and Hobbes were designed to be a comic strip and that's all I want it to be. It's the one place where everything works the way I intend it to" ("Calvin and Hobbes – Art Before Commerce" 2016)

For several years after he stopped Calvin and Hobbes in 1995, the cartoonist did not produce anything available to the public. In June 2014, however, he created three strips for Stephen Pastis's comic strip Pearls Before Swine, featuring a six-year-old girl named Libby.

Earlier that year, Watterson also agreed to an interview for Dave Kellett's documentary "Stripped" which looked at the transition of comics from newspapers to the internet. And he drew the film's poster – a cartoonist jumping out of his clothes in shock!

Youtuber Kristian Williams created a video essay 'Art before Commerce,' which holds that as meaningful art goes, the Calvin and Hobbes comic strip is timeless in its appeal and special because "it didn't give in to crass commercialisation." The introduction to Calvin and Hobbes is always through the comic strips. "If you want Calvin and Hobbes you have to seek it out, it's not going to be shoved down your throat" (Dixit 2016).

Bill Watterson, the creator of the timeless and much-loved comic strip, refuses to commercialise it. Can religious and spiritual people learn from it. Religion and spirituality that touch the most sacred space of human beings, deserve the dignity and honour not to be sold to the highest bidder. It is a pity if religious people have to sell their soul to propagate their religion. Religion too should never be "showed down to your throat."

Religion and spirituality that touch the most sacred space of human beings, deserve the dignity and honour not to be sold to the highest bidder.

20

The Serenity of Silence

One strong pillar of creativity is silence and the serenity it provides to the artist! How can we rediscover silence and serenity in our personal and social lives?

We live in a loud and distracting world, where silence is increasingly awkward to experience. This may be damaging both to our spiritual and physical health.

A 2011 World Health Organization report called noise pollution a "modern plague," concluding that "there is overwhelming evidence that exposure to environmental noise has adverse effects on the health of the population" (Carruthers 2017)

We are continuously filling our ears with music, TV and radio news, podcasts and, of course, the multitude of sounds that we create nonstop in our own heads. Think about it: How many moments each day do you spend in total silence? asks Carolyn Gregoire is a Senior Writer for *The Huffington Post* (Gregoire 500).

As our internal and external environments become louder, more people are beginning to seek out silence, whether through a practice of sitting quietly for 10 minutes every morning or heading off to a 10-day silent retreat.

Gregoire gives four science-backed ways that silence is good for your brain – and how making time for it can make you feel less stressed, more focused and more creative.

1. Silence relieves stress and tension. Florence Nightingale, the 19th-century British nurse wrote that "Unnecessary noise is the most cruel absence of care that can be inflicted on sick or well." Nightingale argued that needless sounds could cause distress, sleep loss and alarm for recovering patients (Gregoire 500).

Just as too much noise can cause stress and tension, research has found that silence has the opposite effect, releasing tension in the brain and body. One scientific article showed that two minutes of silence to be more relaxing than listening to "relaxing" music.

2. Silence replenishes our mental resources. In our everyday lives, sensory input is being thrown at us from every angle. When we can finally get away from these sonic disruptions, our brains' attention centers can restore themselves.

The ceaseless demands of modern life put a significant burden on the prefrontal cortex of the brain, which is involved in high-order thinking, decision-making and problem-solving. Therefore, our attentional resources become drained. When those attention resources are depleted, we become distracted and mentally fatigued and may struggle to focus, solve problems and come up with new ideas.

But according to attention restoration theory, the brain can restore its finite cognitive resources when we are silent. In silence the brain can let down its sensory guard, so to speak.

3. In silence, we can tap into the brain's default mode network. The default mode network of the brain is activated when we engage in what scientists refer to as "self-generated cognition," such as daydreaming, meditating, fantasizing about the future or just letting our minds wander.

When the brain is idle and disengaged from external stimuli, we can finally tap into our inner stream of thoughts, emotions, memories and ideas. Engaging this network helps us to make meaning out of our experiences, empathize with others, be more creative and reflect on our own mental and emotional states (Carruthers 2017).

In order to do this, it is necessary to break away from the distractions that keep us lingering on the shallow surfaces of the mind. Silence is one way of getting there. So, Herman Melville once wrote, "All profound things and emotions of things are preceded and attended by silence" (Gregoire 500).

4. Getting quiet can regenerate brain cells. A 2013 study on mice, involved comparing the effects of ambient noise on the rodents' brains. They found that two hours of silence daily led to the development of new cells in the hippocampus, a key brain region associated with learning, memory and emotion.

Can we rediscover the sanctity and serenity of silence both externally and internally? It can heal us and foster our creativity. It can help us to find God in everything.

Can we rediscover the sanctity and serenity of silence both externally and internally? It can heal us and foster our creativity.

21

Music, Art and Religion

How can we relate art to music and religion? The aesthetic to the religious? What is the logic of art and music?

When we experience art, especially together in a group, we feel connected to something larger. We feel a neural turn-on, which is the "logic of art."

Scientists studying various aspects of the arts believe certain components especially excite the brain. Neuroscientist V.S. Ramachandran proposes several universal laws of art, or common patterns found in works of art across time and cultures. These principles powerfully activate our visual centres. In theory, they tap into evolved survival responses, humans have developed during their biological development. The following common elements are found in famous ballet or orchestra, according to art scholars Sarah L. Kaufman and colleagues writing in *The Washington Times* (*Kaufman 2017*).

a. Isolation: Singling out one element helps the brain block other sensory information and focus attention. This magnifies our emotional reaction, especially when the element is simplified to essentials.

b. Contrast: The brain detects boundaries best when the edges are distinct, especially for objects next to each other.

c. Metaphor: Linking seemingly unrelated elements can heighten emotion and empathy. Our brains create meaning from different artistic movements and this deepens our perception of her pain.

This implies that the body shapes stir different emotions. Neuroscientist Julia F. Christensen and her colleagues at University of London, had subjects rate their emotions triggered by brief, silent videos of ballet dancers, with neither music nor facial expressions to influence them. They found that soft, round and open body shapes elicited positive feelings (*Kaufman 2017).* Edgy body shapes, or spiky, asymmetrical moves, triggered negative emotions, which may be impressive and a little alarming.

In another study, Christensen showed subjects silent dance clips and ones that included music. The subjects wore fingertip sweat-detection devices to monitor their raw emotional responses. In the study, when the music and dance matched – that is, sad music plus sad dancing – the subjects' bodily responses and their reported feelings were stronger.

Something happens when emotionally compatible music and dance combine, which is more powerful than a random combination. In this sense, music becomes the "perfect partner" of the artist.

When we go to the ballet – or any other show – we are entering into a highly controlled experience. If everything works as planned, all the elements contribute to a kind of shared consciousness. In effect, our "billions of brain cells are interacting with billions of other brain cells, busily making the microscopic connections that yoke together the brains of those present with an almost inescapable force" (*Kaufman 2017).*

This happens from the moment we automatically tune ourselves to the audience. Soon we're watching a story unfold that connects us with the performers, vicariously feeling and making meaning out of the actions on stage, responding to the magnetism of specific visual cues, experiencing heightened emotions as music and movement entwine and even bonding with those around us. It is just as the artists – choreographers, directors, playwrights, composers, performers – intended. And this magical transformation starts within the architecture of our brain, writes Kaufman (2017).

Art has emerged from the human brain for tens of thousands of years and every human culture makes it. Yet scientists are only beginning to understand how the brain perceives and produces art and why.

Like so many masterly artworks, the brain remains largely unknown. One secret yet to be discovered is how "the fragile folds of matter locked inside our skulls can not only conceive art, create it and contemplate it, but can also experience being transported by it, out of the head, out of the body, out of space and time and reality itself."

Just like art and music, religious experiences too are intimately connected to the brain. Deeper brain study may help us understand how our brain both enables and limits our collective mystical experiences, like artistic expressions.

Just like art and music, religious experiences too are intimately connected to the brain. Deeper brain study may help us understand how our brain both enables and limits our collective mystical experiences, like artistic expressions.

22

Noel Sheth: Melodies from the Flute

Finally, we shall end this section by focussing on the melodies that flow from the life of a creative individual. Prof. Noel Sheth, who is the embodiment of dialogue and encounter with other religions and culture.

A man of ahimsa, compassion and dialogue! That was, indeed, Prof. Noel Kantilal Sheth SJ. Calm and sober in his attitude, he reached out to others respectfully and reverentially. His meticulous and methodological nature and analytic-synthetic mind made him a humble servant, erudite scholar, efficient teacher and responsible administrator. He had a good eye for details and would plan his personal, professional, academic life extremely meticulously. He reached out to other traditions, religions and cultures with a warm heart and open arms, so that our world may be better and more peaceful place.

He mastered Sanskrit so well that he could authoritatively read and interpret the Indian religious texts. This made him reach out to the Hindu scholars. He also learnt Pali which made him reach out to the Buddhist scholars and devotees. His scholarship enabled him to build bridges between Hinduism, Buddhism and Christianity, so that we could understand and appreciate each other (including our genuine differences and creative diversities) better.

His book, *The Divinity of Krishna* (Sheth 1984) was the result of his doctoral studies in Sanskrit from Harvard University. Prof Noel Sheth SJ passed away on July 8, 2017, sadly and unexpectedly at Bagota, Columbia (local date: July 7). To commemorate meaningfully his 75th birthday (October 31, 2018), his friends, well-wishers and colleagues, decided to bring out this memorial volume. It is aptly titled *Melodies from the Flute: Dialogue between Religions and Cultures - Memorial Volume for Indian Christian Philosopher Rev Noel Sheth SJ.*

This book is about encountering other traditions, building friendly bridges with them, affirming others compassionately, enabling them and appreciating their diversity and difference, through dialogue, interaction and cooperation. The next section of articles delves on the Christian heritage and base that urges to affirm the other. The following section explores the Indian roots of both Prof. Noel Sheth and the readers. The next section on "The Religious Vision," talks of the diversity of religious traditions that is characteristic of India. The next set of articles reflects Noel Sheth's attempts at dialoguing between science and religion. He himself has many articles in this area. The final section explores our life as essentially dialogical (Pandikattu and Karimundackal 2018).

May this book contribute to better harmony among our different religious traditions! May it help us to learn deeply from others' religious traditions and grow in wisdom. May this book be an inspiration to reach out to everyone and everything with compassion, wisdom and love!

Indeed, this book is a tribute to Noel Sheth from his colleagues and friends. We affirm that Noel has tirelessly worked for inter-religious dialogue, has attempted dialogue between science and religion and has assiduously sought for wisdom deeply rooted in our Indian traditions and Christian heritage! So different melodies from the same Flute that is India!

Noel Sheth has tirelessly worked for inter-religious dialogue, has attempted dialogue between science and religion and has assiduously sought for wisdom deeply rooted in our Indian traditions and the Christian heritage!

PART - IV

Deepening Spiritual Practices

23

Does Meditation Make Us Better?

Can creativity, lead to a deeper spirituality? How do we deepen our spiritual encounters and experiences through practices like meditation and prayer? The first essay in this part deals with the usefulness of meditation.

We have been generally assuming that meditation makes humans better, physically, emotionally and spiritually. Does it make us more open to fellow human beings? Does it make us compassionate?

But a recent research suggests that the role of meditation in making us better people is limited. The study by scientists at Coventry University in the UK, Massey University in New Zealand and Radboud University in the Netherlands, reviewed more than 20 studies that investigated the effect of various types of meditation, such as mindfulness and loving-kindness, on pro-social feelings and behaviours. Initial results indicated that meditation did have an overall positive impact, reports Coventry University website (Coventry University 2018).

The researchers said meditation made people feel moderately more compassionate or empathic, compared to if they had done no other new emotionally engaging activity.

However, further analysis revealed that it played no significant role in reducing aggression or prejudice or improving how socially connected someone was. The most unexpected result of this study, though, was that the more positive results found for compassion had significant methodological flaws – compassion levels in some studies only increased if the meditation teacher was also an author of the published report (Coventry University 2018).

Overall, these results suggest that the moderate improvements reported by psychologists in previous studies may be the result of methodological weaknesses and biases, said the researchers. Their research only included randomised controlled studies, where meditators were compared to other individuals who did not meditate.

All these studies used secular meditation techniques derived from Buddhism, such as mindfulness and loving-kindness meditation. Dr Miguel Farias, Reader in Cognitive & Biological Psychology, Coventry University, England, said: "The popularisation of meditation techniques, like mindfulness, despite being taught without religious beliefs, still seem to offer the hope of a better self and a better world to many. We wanted to investigate how powerful these techniques were in affecting one's feelings and behaviours towards others" (Coventry University 2018).

"Despite the high hopes of practitioners and past studies, our research found that methodological shortcomings greatly influenced the results we found. Most of the initial positive results disappeared when the meditation groups were compared to other groups that engaged in tasks unrelated to meditation." He added that the beneficial effect of meditation on compassion disappeared if the meditation teacher was not an author in the studies. This implies that the results might be biased in favour of the teacher leading the meditation.

He also cautions: "None of this, of course, invalidates Buddhism or other religions' claims about the moral value and eventually life-changing potential of its beliefs and practices. But our research findings are a far cry from many popular claims made by meditators and some psychologists."

He adds further: "To understand the true impact of meditation on people's feelings and behaviour further we first need to address the methodological weaknesses we uncovered – starting with the high expectations researchers might have about the power of meditation" (Coventry University 2018).

So the question remains: Does meditation makes us better persons? Does it make us more compassionate? More life-affirming and loving? The research indicates that we need to be more nuanced in our answer.

Obviously, meditation calms our mind and body. It helps us to relax! Does it really change our behaviour? Does it alter the way we deal with fellow human beings? Does it enable us to forgive others, reach out to the less fortunate ones?

In other words, does mediation helps us to encounter the other: be it the other person or God? Or is meditation part of the process of self-talk, giving us only selective positive feedbacks, giving us only a delusory experience of well-being? Any genuine encounter with others or other should shatter our comfort zones and make us more compassionate! It should help us to find God in everything, for a believer. And everything in God! Then it becomes spiritual, with or without God!

Does meditation help us to encounter the other: be it the other person or God? Or is mediation part of the process of self-talk, giving us only selective positive feedbacks, giving us only a delusory experience of well-being? Any genuine encounter with others or Other should shatter our comfort zones and make us more compassionate!

24

Individualised Spirituality

Spiritual experiences are personal individual ones with a necessary reach out to the larger society? How do we evaluate it? How do we measure spirituality? Can we measure the ineffable? The human search for meaning recently took a physical, quantifiable turn as Columbia and Yale University researchers isolated the place in our brains that processes spiritual experiences, writes Ephrat Livni, journalist and lawyer in Quarz (QZ).

In a new study, published May 29, 2018 neuroscientists explain how they generated "personally relevant" spiritual experiences in a diverse group of subjects and scanned their brains while these experiences were happening. The results indicate a "neurobiological home" for spirituality. When we feel a sense of connection with something greater than the self – whether transcendence involves communion with God, nature, or humanity – a certain part of the brain is activated.

The study suggests that there is a "universal, cognitive basis for spirituality, as opposed to a cultural grounding for such states." This new discovery could help improve mental health, according to the researchers (Livni 2018).

Previous studies have examined the brain activity of Buddhist monks or Catholic nuns. But the present research analyzed subjects from different backgrounds with varying degrees of religiosity and totally different individual notions of what constitutes a spiritual experience.

"Although studies have linked specific brain measures to aspects of spirituality, none have sought to directly examine spiritual experiences," particularly using a broader, modern understanding of spirituality, the researchers explain. Because there are many types of transcendent moments with varying degrees of meaning to different people, it is been difficult to test the general effects of spirituality, as opposed to religiosity. So for this study, the researchers generated individual scripts that put each subject in their own relevant transcendent state.

With each of the 27 subjects, the researchers created a personal script based on each person's self-reported previous spiritual experiences. The scientists then scanned brain activity when generating such a state in the subjects.

During their varied transcendent states, all subjects showed similar activity patterns in the parietal cortex, which processes sensation, spatial orientation and language and is thought to influence attention, among other functions.

The effect on the brain is distinct from the effect of other forms of relaxation, according to researchers. "We observed in the spiritual condition, as compared with the neutral-relaxing condition, reduced activity in the left inferior parietal lobule (IPL), a result that suggests the IPL may contribute importantly to perceptual processing and self-other representations during spiritual experiences," the study explains (Livni 2018).

These changes in the brain may help explain why, during spiritual experiences, the barrier between the self and others can be reduced or even eliminated altogether. Although we need some separation between ourselves and everyone else for protection and to manage reality, removing the barrier is also valuable.

"Spiritual experiences are robust states that may have profound impacts on people's lives," explains Yale psychiatry and neuroscience professor Marc Potenza. "Understanding the neural bases of spiritual experiences may help us better understand their roles in resilience and recovery from mental health and addictive disorders."

Such experiences involve "pronounced shifts in perception [that] buffer the effects of stress," the study says. The findings suggest that those experiences can be accessed by everyone and that transcendence is not dependent upon religiosity. That makes studying spiritual experiences and figuring out how to use such states for improved mental health easier for scientists (Livni 2018).

Beyond mental health, scientists study spirituality because of the universal human quest for meaning. By cultivating spiritual experiences in addition to strengthening our intellectual abilities, people can lead emotionally richer lives and develop more open minds, scientists say.

It is beneficial to evolve an individualized and quantified spirituality. But we also need to remember that everything cannot be quantified. Spirituality has a necessary social component, which must reach out to the other! Spirituality cannot also be reduced to its beneficial or "selfish" aspects!

> Beyond mental health, scientists study spirituality because of the universal human quest for meaning. By cultivating spiritual experiences in addition to strengthening our intellectual abilities, people can lead emotionally more productive lives and develop more open minds.

25

Mindfulness Meditation

In this section, we turn our attention to mindfulness meditation. We ask ourselves: How cannot invasive meditation make us more holistic and harmonious?

There is currently no known way to prevent older adults with mild cognitive impairment (MCI) from developing Alzheimer's disease. But there may be a safe and feasible non-pharmacological treatment that may help patients living with MCI, according to a small pilot study in the current issue of the *Journal of Alzheimer's Disease* led by a neurologist and researcher with Wake Forest Baptist Health, North Carolina, USA (Wake Forest Baptist Medical Center 2019).

"Until treatment options that can prevent the progression to Alzheimer's are found, mindfulness meditation may help patients living with MCI," said Rebecca Erwin Wells, M.D., M.P.H., Associate Professor of Neurology at Wake Forest School of Medicine, a practising neurologist at Wake Forest Baptist Medical Center and associate director of clinical research for its Center for Integrative Medicine. "Our study showed promising evidence that adults with MCI can learn to practice mindfulness meditation and by doing so may boost their cognitive reserve."

Mindfulness means maintaining a moment-by-moment, non-judgmental awareness of thoughts, feelings, bodily sensations and surrounding environment, reports *ScienceDaily*.

"While the concept of mindfulness meditation is simple, the practice itself requires complex cognitive processes, discipline and commitment," Wells explained. "This study suggests that the cognitive impairment in MCI is not prohibitive of what is required to learn this new skill."

Research has demonstrated that high levels of chronic stress negatively impact the hippocampus, a part of the brain involved in memory and learning and are associated with increased incidence of MCI and Alzheimer's. Other studies have indicated that non-drug interventions such as aerobic exercise can have positive effects on cognition, stress levels and the brain.

To test whether a mindfulness-based stress-reduction (MBSR) program could benefit adults with MCI, the study team enlisted 14 men and women between the ages of 55 and 90 with clinically diagnosed MCI and randomized them to either an eight-week course involving mindfulness meditation and yoga or a "waiting list" control group (Wake Forest Baptist Medical Center 2019).

The researchers previously reported that the nine participants who completed the MBSR program showed trends toward improvements on measures of cognition and well-being and indications of positive impacts on the hippocampus as well as other areas of the brain associated with cognitive decline.

The newly published study adds context to those quantitative findings with a qualitative analysis of the MBSR participants' responses in interviews conducted at the end of the eight-week course.

"While the MBSR course was not developed or structured to directly address MCI, the qualitative interviews revealed new and important findings specific to MCI," Wells said. "The participants' comments and ratings showed that most of them were able to learn the key tenets of mindfulness, demonstrating that the memory impairment of MCI does not preclude learning such skills" (Wake Forest Baptist Medical Center 2019).

Those participants who practiced at least 20 minutes a day were most likely to have understood the underlying concepts of mindfulness, Wells noted.

The limitations of the study include the small sample size and that the results may not generalise to all patients with MCI, as two-thirds of the participants in this study had a college education or more. Additional research is needed to test further the preliminary hypotheses contained in this study.

We know that in general meditation can calm us down. The above study suggests that mindfulness meditation, which is not invasive, can make us more holistic and harmonious. That may heal us and make us healthier – physically and mentally.

> "The participants' comments and ratings showed that most of them were able to learn the key tenets of mindfulness, demonstrating that the memory impairment of mild cognitive impairment does not preclude learning such skills"

26

Digital Meditation

Can classical meditation be enhanced by contemporary digital technology? Surprisingly, some positive results emerge from some recent experiments. Scientists at University of California, San Francisco, have developed a personalized digital meditation training program that significantly improved attention and memory in healthy young adults – a group already at the peak of brain health – in just six weeks (University of California 2019).

The intervention, called 'MediTrain', utilizes a closed-loop algorithm that tailors the length of the meditation sessions to the abilities of the participants, so they are not discouraged by their initial attempts to focus attention on their breath, a time-honoured meditation technique.

Scientists tested the program in a randomized, double-blind, placebo-controlled trial at UCSF with 59 participants between 18 and 35 years old. The results were published Monday, June 3, 2019, in *Nature Human Behaviour* (University of California 2019).

The magnitude of the effects on attention and memory, which were unexpected for healthy young adults, were like what has been seen in previous studies of middle-aged adults after months of in-person training or intensive meditation retreats.

The app-based program, however, required just 20 to 30 minutes of cumulative practice each day, composed of many noticeably short meditation periods. In the beginning, participants were prompted to pay attention to their breath for just 10 to 15 seconds at a time. As they improved over the six weeks, the application challenged them to increase the amount of time they could maintain focus, which averaged several minutes after six weeks.

"This is not like any meditation practice that exists, as far as we are aware," said senior author Adam Gazzaley, MD, PhD, professor of neurology, physiology and psychiatry and executive director of Neuroscape at UCSF. "We took an ancient experiential treatment of focused meditation, reformulated it and delivered it through digital technology and improved attention span in millennials, an age group that is intimately familiar with the digital world, but also faces multiple challenges to sustained attention" (University of California 2019).

MediTrain made some concessions to tradition. Before they began, participants listened to recorded meditation instructions from Jack Kornfield, PhD, a meditation teacher who co-founded Spirit Rock Meditation Center north of San Francisco and an author on the study. Then, they used the techniques on their own, without spoken instruction and with their eyes closed.

But MediTrain had other digital features that are not present in the traditional practice of breath meditation that may have been the reason why it achieved such strong results over such a short period and with such a healthy population.

For one thing, it underscored the need to pay attention by requiring participants to regularly check in on how they were faring.

At the end of each brief meditation segment, participants were asked to indicate whether they had been able to pay continuous attention for the allotted time, pressing a button on the left side of an iPad screen if the answer was no and a button on the right if the answer was yes. For those who said yes, the application adapted to a slightly longer meditation period; for those who said no, the period was shortened.

"Not only do you learn how to maintain focus on your breath, but you are also required to introspect on how well you're able to do that," Gazzaley said, "We believe that's part of the active ingredient of this treatment."

MediTrain also gave everyone regular feedback, with progress reports during the training sessions, at the end of each day of training and at the end of each week.

The results were impressive. On their first day, participants could stay focused on their breath for an average of only 20 seconds. After 30 days of training, that rose to an average of six minutes.

This improvement, in turn, conferred better performance on other, much more complicated tasks that scientists use to assess sustained attention and working memory. Not only did the MediTrain participants perform more consistently on attention tests than the placebo group, the scientists also found a correlation between how long participants were able to focus on their breath and how consistently they performed on these tests. The MediTrain group also performed better than the placebo group on a test of working memory, measured after the intervention (University of California 2019).

"We thought it was a long shot to see these types of improvements in a group this young and healthy," said David Ziegler, PhD, director of multimodal biosensing in the technology division at UCSF's Neuroscape and the first author of the paper. "But it speaks to the power of the method."

The researchers said that MediTrain, which has been patented by the University of California, holds promise for a younger generation that is accustomed to digital devices but faces multiple challenges to sustained attention from heavy use of media and technology.

The breath meditation – a seemingly simple, yet quite demanding task – worked as well in cultivating sustained attention as other more intellectually and physically challenging training programs that have been developed at Neuroscape, a translational neuroscience center at UCSF engaged in technology creation and scientific research to better assess and optimize brain function for all people.

"Many of us struggle with challenges to our attention, which seem to be exacerbated by modern technology," Gazzaley said. "What we've done here is flip this story around by creating and studying a digital delivery system that makes cognitive benefits of traditional focused attention meditation more personalized, accessible and deliverable."

> "We took an ancient experiential treatment of focused meditation, reformulated it and delivered it through a digital technology and improved attention span in millennials, an age group that is intimately familiar with the digital world, but also faces multiple challenges to sustained attention"

27

Politics and Spirituality

Spirituality cannot be separated from life and from politics. In this article, we see how one individual, a politician, tries to present her spiritual views to a political audience.

Author, activist and faith leader Marianne Williamson recently burst onto the political scene as a somewhat unconventional candidate vying for the Democratic Party's presidential nomination in the United States.

What distinguishes Williamson from other candidates is her personal and professional background. Prior to her foray into politics, she was an internationally renowned self-help and spiritual author and speaker, known for penning bestsellers like *A Return to Love*.

A child of the 1960s, Williamson was significantly involved with the New Age and Human Potential movements, even spending time working. Today, she is known as Oprah Winfrey's spiritual adviser and remains an outspoken advocate of mindfulness meditation, yoga and therapy as ways to achieve spiritual and social transformation (Watts 2019).

Williamson unapologetically infuses her interest in spirituality into her political campaigning and calls for a spiritual awakening. On her website she calls for "a moral and spiritual awakening" in America, speaking to those who are "seeking higher wisdom." And in her closing statement at the first Democratic debate, she proclaimed that she would harness love to defeat President Donald Trump.

We have seen a dramatic rise over the last few decades in the number of North Americans who self-identify as "spiritual but not religious." Those in this group, while certainly diverse, have deep spiritual interests, often champion something like the existence of a higher power, remain wary of orthodoxy and place a premium on individual autonomy.

It is these people to whom Williamson appeals. And while they might view themselves as seekers who do not adhere to traditions, there is a longstanding tradition of alternative spirituality in the West.

In *Spiritual but not Religious: Understanding Unchurched America,* religious historian Robert Fuller (2010) sheds light on the various metaphysical movements that emerged in the 18th and 19th centuries in America (Watts 2019).

These movements were certainly theologically different, but nevertheless, like Williamson and her followers, they postulated the existence of unseen forces and championed the importance of both mystical experiences and individual freedom. If channelled appropriately, those forces could purportedly lead to self-empowerment.

The influence of these movements was far from marginal in American society. They often attracted well-known writers, politicians and artists. Ralph Waldo Emerson, often called America's national poet and avowed Transcendentalist, as was Henry Thoreau, committed civil rights activist and author. Others who belonged to some of these movements include psychologists William James and Carl Jung, philosopher Rudolf Steiner and biologist Alfred Russell Wallace.

The spiritual is political: Historian Leigh Eric Schmidt of Princeton University usefully traces the historical ties between these movements and progressive democratic politics in the U.S. in *Restless Souls: The Making of American Spirituality* (Schmidt 2012). Schmidt observes that many of the leaders and spokespeople of these movements were ahead of their time, both socially and politically. Walt Whitman, the famous American poet and writer spoke of "the good in all religious systems," according to Schmidt.

Felix Adler (2019), a Reform Jew and founder of the Society for Ethical Culture, published in 1905 *The Essential Spirituality*, wherein he championed the importance of "doing justice to that inner self" in order to do "justice to others."

Considering this history, Schmidt concludes: "The convergence of political progressivism, socioeconomic justice and mystical interiority was at the heart of the rise of a spiritual left in American culture" (Watts 2019).

It is therefore worth asking why a candidate like Williamson so boggles the modern-day mind. In part, it has to do with the way alternative spirituality developed over the 20th century. The New Age movement of the 1970s was arguably the most prominent. And while the "New Age" label may today be out of fashion, many ideas that were once championed under its banner remain strikingly popular.

In fact, it is likely that many who call themselves "spiritual but not religious" subscribe to a set of ideas and engage in a variety of practices that were once central to that counter-cultural movement. And carrying forward a long-standing tradition, these ideas tend to appeal to the left. They are both political and spiritual.

"The convergence of political progressivism, socioeconomic justice and mystical interiority was at the heart of the rise of a spiritual left in American culture"

28

Thadam Chundamthadam: *Fully Spiritual, Fully Human*

Spirituality implies not another-worldly withdrawal, but a full immersion into this world of our human beings. This was the view of Dr Stephen Thadam, who has implemented a two year Master's Programme in Spirituality at Jnana Deepa (JD), Pune.

The mystery of incarnation is commonly understood as the mystery of human being's divinization because it tells us that a man, Jesus of Nazareth, became the Son of God. Therefore, when we say that God became human in Jesus, we are saying that God can be found in everything truly human. Moreover, it impels us to place our faith in everything that is human because it not possible to find God outside humankind. Thus, the mystery of incarnation brings the divinity and humanity together and sets a challenge to develop a spirituality that humanizes (Karimundackal and Pandikattu 2019).

However, being 'spiritual' is often thought to be superior to being 'human' and thus minimizes the value of being human, which we all are. Often cited a quotation attributed to Teilhard de Chardin further misconstrue that we should be more spiritual than human: "We are not human beings having a spiritual experience. We are spiritual beings having a human experience." Since some of us see being spiritual as incongruent with being human, we may develop a disconnect with our humanness, which will limit our spiritual growth by going into 'spiritual bypass' to avoid our human issues.

Since time immemorial 'spirituality' has been a way of being that is above and beyond our 'faulty' humanness. Interestingly, the Webster's Dictionary distinguishes being spiritual from being human, defining spirituality as, that which is "concerned with or affecting the spirit or soul," "lacking material body or form or substance… the vital transcendental soul belonging to the spiritual realm," "of or pertaining to the moral feelings or states of the soul," and "of or pertaining to the soul or its affections as influenced by the spirit… proceeding from the holy spirit; pure; holy; divine; heavenly-minded; opposed to carnal." This kind of understanding of spirituality bypasses all the challenges of the human experience. How long we will take to get away from the idea that spirituality and humanness are two different realms, one higher or more meaningful than the other?

We are not only "spiritual beings having a human experience," but also human beings having a spiritual experience. If we do not accept this, we may be desacralizing our own 'self', thinking that it is something less than sacred and divine. If we do not believe that what happens to us as 'human' is spiritually relevant, we will not take efforts to improve our own behaviour or become more inclusive in our living and thinking; we will not worry about human rights violations or creating social and political structures that enhance our sacred significance and our living together here on this planet. From this vantage point, we cannot ignore the needs of humanity because we understand that everything is sacred. It is time for us to nurture a spirituality that is not dualistic, not other worldly, not fear based, not cultic, but life-affirming, compassionate, joy-giving and celebrating the simple things of life.

Rev. Stephen C. Thadam has been actively involved in promoting a spirituality that is both human and spiritual. As the founding director of the Center for Spirituality at Jnana Deepa (JD), Pontifical Athenaeum of Philosophy and Religion, Pune, he stressed for an integrated spirituality programme for the spirituality programmes in Jnana Deepa (JD). Besides his expertise in Indian Philosophy, especially in *Vedanta,* he has focused on the rich spiritual traditions of other Indian religions. Training the young in Yoga and Karate was his passion. He has seriously engaged in giving meditations and retreats to the young and old, to the lay faithful and religious alike. He reached out to others respectfully and reverentially. For him spirituality and humanness are not two different realms, one higher or more meaningful than the other, but an integrated divine-human convergence. This special volume is a token of our gratitude to him. Through this book, we acknowledge his contribution not only to the Indian philosophy and Indian Church but also at the personal level. He has personally touched and inspired us (Karimundackal and Pandikattu 2019).

So the book *Fully Spiritual, Fully Human: Essays in Honour of Dr Stephen Chundamthadam SJ Fostering Diverse Spiritual Experiences* (Karimundackal and Pandikattu 2019) brought out by his colleagues to honour this great spiritual person, whom we can consider both as a visionary and a mystic.

> Spirituality and humanness are not two different realms, one higher or more meaningful than the other, but an integrated divine-human convergence.

29

Mother Teresa: Saint of Darkness

Spirituality does not always guarantee happiness and fullness. Emptiness and darkness are part of being spiritual. The example of Mother Teresa, a true spiritual mystic. "I am told God lives in me – and yet the reality of darkness and coldness and emptiness is so great that nothing touches my soul." wrote Mother Teresa in 1957. Mother Teresa, who is proclaimed a saint, wrestled with a sense of God's absence for the last 50 years of her life (Scott 2013). In 2007, *Come Be My Light (*Teresa and Kolodiejchuk 2014), a book that collected many of her most personal and private correspondence, was published. It immediately caused confusion in her admirers and glee in her detractors.

Her private letters revealed that, except for one short period, Teresa had been afflicted with a deep sense of God's absence for the last half-century of her life. There is no sense in denying that Mother Teresa's sojourn in the wilderness is deeply disconcerting. If God can seem absent to a saint like her, what chance do the rest of us have to connect with God? Asks Kerry Walters (2016a), professor of philosophy, in his *St. Teresa of Calcutta: Missionary, Mother, Mystic.*

Such a sense of abandonment is part of every mystical tradition. For the Spanish mystic, John of the Cross, or "dark night of the soul" is a forlorn feeling of being abandoned by God. "Both the sense and the spirit," he writes, "as though under an immense and dark load, undergo such agony and pain that the soul would consider death a relief." The soul suffers most from the conviction that "God has rejected it and with abhorrence cast it into darkness" (Walters 2016).

For Mother, the painful sense of being rejected by God is a purification of the senses and spirit that prepares the way for an "inflow of God into the soul." There is no set time limit for a dark night of the soul, although most do not last as long as Mother Teresa's did. Nor does the dark night mean that the sufferer has ceased to believe in God, although intense doubts can arise.

In one of her letters, Mother Teresa writes, "In my soul I feel just that terrible pain of loss – of God not wanting me – of God not being God – of God not really existing." Her suffering when God hid from her was intense. Her private correspondence to her confessors attests to that. She notes: "In the darkness…Lord, my God, who am I that You should forsake me?... The one You have thrown away as unwanted – unloved. I call, I cling, I want – and there is no One to answer – no One on. Whom I can cling? – no, No One. Alone. The darkness is so dark – and I am alone."

What bewildered her very much was that the darkness had descended in 1949, right when she believed she was precisely doing the work God had created her to do. Her loss of the presence of God coincided with the granting of the long-sought permission to found the order that became the Missionaries of Charity, notes Walters.

But in 1958 she writes: "There and then disappeared that long darkness, that pain of loss – of loneliness – of that strange suffering of ten years. Today my soul is filled with love." But in just a short time, God "thought it better for me to be in the tunnel – so He is gone again." Teresa would endure the tunnel for the next four decades. In 1962, in the second decade of her sense of abandonment, Teresa wrote something prophetic: "If I ever become a saint – I will surely be one of 'darkness.' I will continually be absent from heaven – to light the light of those in darkness on earth."

We need to realise that sometimes we can find God only in his agonizing absence and in the darkness of our depravity! Genuine spirituality is not comfortable.

"If I ever become a saint – I will surely be one of 'darkness.' I will continually be absent from heaven – to light the light of those in darkness on earth."

30

Julian of Norwich: All Shall be Well

Another mystic, who unwaveringly instils hope in our contemporary situation. Hope in the darkest hour possible! For spirituality breeds joy and hope, even in the most tragic environment.

In her life Julian of Norwich (1342-1416) suffered intensely. She grew up in a world ravaged by the Hundred Years' War between England and France. She lived through the Peasants' Revolt in 1381, during which thousands of disenfranchised tenant farmers and labourers marched all over England looting monasteries, burning records of their serfdom and debt and killing their hated overlords. Most tragic of all, from the time Julian was six years old, she endured repeated outbreaks of the Great Pestilence - the Black Death - which eventually killed more than half the population of Europe, some *50 million* people (Rolf 2019).

When Julian was 30, her body broke down. She became paralyzed and was near death. The local curate told her to fix her eyes on the crucifix. Suddenly all her pain was taken away and the figure of Christ on the cross appeared to come alive. For the next 12 hours, Julian entered a profound mystical experience of Christ's sufferings and his transformation into glory. She received sixteen revelations and heard locutions that stayed with her for the rest of her life - especially Christ's personal reassurance that

"Alle shalle be wele and alle shalle be wele and all manner of thing shalle be wele" (Rolf 2019).

Julian could not accept these words at first. How could she believe that 'all things would be well' when her own world was obviously falling apart? She was so tortured by the success of evil and the degradation of suffering that she had often wondered why "the beginning of sin had not been prevented. For then I thought all would have been wele." She dared to question the vision: "Ah, good lord, *how* might alle be wele for the great harm that has come by sin to thy creatures?" Julian's mental anguish was indicative of humanity's innate sense that our lives are terribly broken and that we do not know how to fix them. We simply cannot save ourselves from the messes we get into because of our pride, anger, selfishness, jealousy, greed and lies.

Surprisingly, Julian was told that sin could be "behovely" - that is, "useful," even "necessary"- because it forces us to realize our need for divine mercy and spiritual healing. She further understood that in God there is no wrath or blame - all the anger and recrimination are on *our* side. God shows only compassion and pity for human beings because of the inevitable suffering we must endure as a result of our misdeeds. Julian became convinced that everyone is loved unconditionally by God.

> *So she wrote: "For our soul is so preciously loved by him that is highest, that it overpasses the knowing of all creatures: that is to say, there is no creature that is made that may know how much and how sweetly and how tenderly our maker loves us...And therefore we may ask of our lover, with reverence, all that we will." (Rolf 2019).*

This revelation filled Julian with immense compassion for her fellow human beings. She longed to bear witness to divine love, mercy and the revelations she had experienced. There were three things she decided to do: *pray, counsel and write.*

Around 1390, Julian chose to be enclosed as an anchorite - literally "anchored" to the side of the church. There she lived for about 25 years in a small hermit's cell, attended by a maid who brought her food, clean clothing, parchment and ink. She devoted herself to prayer and contemplation, to counseling those who came to her anchorage window seeking spiritual direction and to writing.

She realized that "as truly as God is our father, as truly is God our mother." By giving birth to humankind in blood and water on the cross and by nurturing and inspiring us throughout our lives, Mother Christ is the paradigm for all earthly mothers, caregivers, advisors, teachers and volunteers; for all those who dedicate their lives to the works of mercy and social service. All the while, Julian searched for the deeper meaning of all the Lord's revelations. One day she was answered in prayer: "Know it well, love was his meaning." Divine love became the meaning of her life and her message to the world (Rolf 2019).

Although Julian was, by her own account, "unlettered" (she could not read or write Latin, the language of Scripture and theology), she was the first woman ever to write a book in the English language.

It was not until 1910 that the Short Text finally resurfaced. Since then, Julian's reputation and influence have grown worldwide. The American mystic and activist Thomas Merton called Julian one of "the greatest English theologians," and former Archbishop of Canterbury Rowan Williams considered Julian's book to be "the most important work of Christian reflection in the English language."

How can we work to make 'all things well' in our world without losing heart, like Julian? Without falling into the twin dangers of disillusionment and burnout. Julian would tell us that we must go into the "ground" of our being in order to "live contemplatively." Like her, we must develop a daily practice in which we learn to rest and breathe in silence and stillness, becoming aware of the turbulence in our minds, releasing thoughts and letting go of our emotional attachment to those thoughts.

Such practice will transform *us*. Our love will go deeper, our patience will grow stronger and our service will become more authentic and productive. We will be able to feel compassion for those who challenge us and keep our balance in situations that threaten to undermine us. We will listen more attentively, evaluate opposing viewpoints more generously and cooperate more willingly. We will recognize that the real work of transformation is *divine* work. Nevertheless, we humans play an indispensable part: every act of peace and service and every word of kindness or forgiveness helps to make "alle manner of thing" well.

"Alle shalle be wele and alle shalle be wele and all manner of thing shalle be wele"

PART - V

Nurturing the Aesthetic

31

Becoming Conscious of Oneself

After deepening our spiritual experience, we turn to the aesthetic or the beautiful. How does beauty help us to appreciate not just the beautiful things around us, but our own selves? How does beauty lead us to the Divine? How does the sense of beauty make us more sympathetic?

We first begin with our self-consciousness. What is the role of creative consciousness in our lives? How can it change our life? How can we consciously live and transform our surroundings? These issues are taken up by the world-famous author Eckhart Tolle (2018) in his classic, *The Power of Now.*

Tolle says that with the acknowledgement and acceptance of the facts also comes a degree of freedom from them. For example, when we know there is disharmony and you hold that "knowing," through our knowing a new factor has come in and the disharmony cannot remain unchanged. When we know we are not at peace, our knowing creates a still space that surrounds your non-peace in a loving and tender embrace and then transmutes your non-peace into peace. As far as inner transformation is concerned, there is nothing we can do about it. "You cannot transform yourself and you certainly cannot transform your partner or anybody else. All you can do is create a space for transformation to happen, for grace and love to enter," says Tolle (2018).

So whenever our relationship is not working, whenever it brings out the "madness" in us and in our partner, we can be glad. "What was unconscious is being brought up to the light. It is an opportunity for salvation." Every moment hold the knowing of that moment, particularly of our inner state. If there is anger, we can realise that there is anger. If there is jealousy, defensiveness, the urge to argue, the need to be right, an inner child demanding love and attention, or emotional pain of any kind – whatever it is, we can know the reality of that moment and hold the knowing.

The relationship then becomes our *sadhana*, our spiritual practice. If we observe unconscious behaviour in our partner or friend, Tolle suggests that we hold it in the loving embrace of knowing so that we do not react negatively. He reminds us that unconsciousness and knowing cannot coexist for long – even if the knowing is only in the other person and not in the one who is acting out the unconsciousness. The energy form that lies behind hostility and attack finds the presence of love intolerable. If we react at all to our partner's unconsciousness, we become unconscious ourselves. But if we then remember to know your reaction, nothing is lost.

Tolle tells us that "humanity is under great pressure to evolve because it is our only chance of survival as a race" (Tolle 2018) This will affect every aspect of our life and close relationships. "Never before have relationships been as problematic and conflict ridden as they are now." Most people are there not to make you happy or fulfilled. "If you continue to pursue the goal of salvation through a relationship, you will be disillusioned again and again," he warns. But if we accept that the relationship is here to make us conscious instead of happy, then the relationship can offer us salvation and we will be aligning ourselves with the "higher consciousness that wants to be born into this world" (Tolle 2018).

Tolle is right in reminding ourselves that relationship alone cannot solve our human misery. Just like in other areas of life, relationship has so many nuances and grey areas. By becoming conscious of them we can transform ourselves and the larger society. If we can genuinely relate to the other, despite their weakness and even wickedness, then we can change ourselves and the larger society.

In fact, most of world's problems boil down to relationship between individuals and groups. The only way to make ourselves happy and to preserve human survival is by fostering a better or deeper relationship. For that we need to promote consciousness affirmation and acceptance of the other, even in their wickedness!

Relationship alone cannot solve our human misery. Just like in other areas of life, relationship has so many nuances and grey areas. By becoming conscious of them we can transform ourselves and the larger society. If we can genuinely relate to the other, despite their weakness and even wickedness, then we can change ourselves and the larger society.

32

Remaining Absolutely Curious

Leading physicist and Italian author Carlo Rovelli (2019), has authored a fascinating book, *The Order of Time*. It is about the history of our understanding of time. He brings the reader on a historical journey, from Aristotle to Einstein and beyond into the 21st century where today quantum mechanics is heavily involved. Rovelli also has an interest in philosophy and he hints at what the emerging ideas about time might mean for human existence.

In an exclusive interview to science journalist Conor Purcell, **he dwelt on** the main message of the book: the concept that time can no longer be understood as a single notion. Part of the reason for this is that we human beings – because of our size – can only observe macroscopic variables and not the microphysics of things. So, the observations we make are clearly time-oriented, but only because there is heat involved; time orientation is related to heat and statistical mechanics (Purcell 2018).

Putting it all together, our perception of time is related to this macroscopic perspective, the idea that we can only see a statistical view, rather than the world as it really is. But time itself would disappear at the molecular level, where the past and future become equally determinable – meaning there would be no apparent difference between past and future.

He elaborates **"rebellion is perhaps among the deepest roots of science: the refusal to accept the present order of things".** He comes from that generation which in the late 1960s and early 1970s was very much rebellious. It was a time of big dreams, with intentions of building a more just world. He elaborates: "I was immersed in that culture. To some extent it was a failed revolution – the world did not go in that direction at all. So, at one time there was a moment in my life when I became disappointed by that and in that moment, I fell in love with science. What attracted me was that in science you can make real change – you can make revolution, in ways that can be even easier than in the "real" world of politics. In fact, in science you must make revolution in order to see further than before" (Purcell 2018).

Later during his university years, while studying general relativity and eventually quantum mechanics, he realised that this stuff is better than drugs – better than LSD. He found the problem of quantum gravity so fascinating and "right there and then I knew that I wanted to study it for the rest of my life. I have since done so and I feel that it is a privilege to be involved in science, doing what I love to do" (Purcell 2018).

He acknowledges that one of the reasons people buy his books is because he talks of science and of God. He is an atheist because he knows he does not know, unlike many theists. "Not because I think I know the answers and that people who believe in God don't know them. It's because I know that I don't know the answers and I am aware of this ignorance. I don't think there should be arrogance in pretending to know everything and I struggle to understand how people can be so sure they know about God. For some people it comes natural to think there must be something behind it all" (Purcell 2018).

He adds: "What is very typical of science is that the more we learn the more we don't know. I don't think it's disconcerting. I don't think anyone knows where the universe came from and I think we just have to accept that. We must accept to live at least partly in ignorance, but nevertheless remain absolutely curious" (Purcell 2018). Always! Everywhere! Absolutely curious! About ourselves and the world!

> "What is very typical of science is that the more we learn the more we don't know. I don't think it's disconcerting. I don't think anyone knows where the universe came from and I think we just have to accept that. We must accept to live at least partly in ignorance, but nevertheless remain absolutely curious"

33

The Dangers of Curiosity

How is curiosity part of our openness to the beautiful? Is curiosity always positive? Does it always lead to noble ends? We regard curiosity as positive and a powerful motivator, as indicated in the previous essay. New research shows that our curiosity is sometimes so powerful that it leads us to choose potentially painful and unpleasant outcomes that have no apparent benefits, even when we have the ability to avoid these outcomes altogether.

"Just as curiosity drove Pandora to open the box despite being warned of its pernicious contents, curiosity can lure humans to seek information with predictably ominous consequences," explains study author Bowen Ruan of the Wisconsin School of Business at the University of Wisconsin-Madison (Association for Psychological Science 2016)..

Ruan and co-author Christopher Hsee at the University of Chicago Booth School of Business assumed that this curiosity stems from humans' deep-seated desire to resolve uncertainty regardless of the harm it may bring. To test this hypothesis, they designed a series of experiments that exposed participants to a variety of particularly unpleasant outcomes, as reported in *ScienceDaily*, April 8, 2016 (Association for Psychological Science 2016).

In one study, 54 college student participants came to the lab and were shown electric-shock pens that were supposedly leftover from a previous experiment; they were told that they could click the pens to kill time while they waited for the "real" study task to begin.

For some of the participants, the pens were colour-coded according to whether they would deliver a shock to another person – five pens that would shock had a red sticker and five pens that wouldn't shock had a green sticker – meaning that the students knew with certainty what would happen when they clicked a given pen.

Other participants, however, saw 10 pens that all bore yellow stickers and were told that some of the pens had batteries while others did not. In this case, the outcome of clicking each pen was uncertain.

The results showed that students in the uncertain condition clicked noticeably more pens. On average, those who did not know what the outcome would be clicked about five pens, while those who knew the outcome clicked about one green pen and two red pens (Association for Psychological Science 2016).

A second study, in which students were shown 10 pens of each colour, confirmed these results. Once again, students clicked more of the uncertain outcome pens than the pens that were clearly identified.

To find out whether the findings would hold under other conditions and whether resolving curiosity would indeed make participants feel worse, the researchers designed a third study involving exposure to pleasant and unpleasant sounds. Participants saw a computer display of 48 buttons, each of which played a sound when clicked. Buttons labelled "nails" would play a sound of nails on a chalkboard, buttons labelled "water" played a sound of running water and buttons labelled "?" had an equal chance of playing either sound. It was found that students who saw mostly uncertain buttons clicked about 39 buttons, while those who saw mostly identified buttons clicked only about 28 (Association for Psychological Science 2016).

Interestingly, the results also showed that participants who clicked more buttons reported feeling worse afterwards and those who faced mostly uncertain outcomes reported being less happy. It was evident that participants faced with uncertain outcomes clicked on more pictures (and felt worse overall); but when they could predict how they would feel about their choice first, they clicked on relatively fewer pens (and felt happier overall).

The findings make a significant point: "While curiosity is often seen as a human blessing, it can also be a human curse. Many times, we seek out information to satisfy our curiosity without considering what will happen when we do." Ruan and Hsee concludes: "Curious people do not always perform consequentialist cost-benefit analyses and may be tempted to seek the missing information even when the outcome is expectedly harmful" (Association for Psychological Science 2016). Unfettered curiosity may also lead to dangerous situations. Always and absolutely curious. But let us also realise our own inherent limits!

"Curious people do not always perform consequentialist cost-benefit analyses and may be tempted to seek the missing information even when the outcome is expectedly harmful" Unfettered curiosity may also lead to dangerous situations.

34

The Art and Authenticity of Writing

The sense of the beautiful reaches out to the writing. We see in this section the relationship between written materials and beauty.

As all of us know, in today's world, visual storytelling of every conceivable variety is booming worldwide. In scope and volume the visual images and movies surpass written and static words. Can we give up on reading and writing? Can we be better off tuning into the mass media? Will the technological revolution take us back to the oral tradition? Is it a healthy trend?

Less writing has become trendy today. Examples include the diminishment of fiction in the common core curriculum, the ever-rising culture of computer games and the blockbuster movies filled with special effects geared towards children and teenagers. Nor must we ignore the economic dangers that lie ahead for the written word. The narrative film industry is a moneymaker that dwarfs the publishing industry currently in the throes of financial revolution and disorder. As the distribution channels of the written word lose traction, the danger to its economic survival will become more and more evident (Adler 2015).

The other underlying question, of course, is does it really matter if the written word bows to the world of film/TV? Novelist and writer Warren Adler holds that "any diminishment of fiction delivered by words is a loss for mankind and must be confronted."

There is no greater human attribute than the imagination. It lies at the very soul of the human species. It is the brain's most powerful engine. It is the essential muscle of life and like all muscles, it must be exercised and perpetually strengthened.

"Writing and reading are the principal tools that inspire, create and empower our imagination without which we are bereft, muted and lesser. Anything that diminishes that power is the enemy of mankind," says Adler (2015).

Adler is not categorically opposed to the myriad manifestations of new media and technological advances. We need to adapt to evolving technology and modes of distribution. The other forms of communication and art must be embraced. So, Adler hopes that "the written word will only stand to be enhanced and complemented by its visual counterparts, not pushed to the brink of extinction."

Writing in *The Huffington Post*, Adler, author of *Torture Man* (2015a) pleads for a greater, not a lesser emphasis on the written word "as the paramount storytelling device ever invented for human communication beyond speech itself" (Adler 2015).

Words conjure more profound and more creative possibilities of thought and interpretation than what is pre-packaged for our consideration. The heart of storytelling is the ultimate quest for "what happens next," which motivates us to contemplate our mortality.

Herein Adler sees "the mystery of all human life, a necessary component of our existence." This leads us to ask the questions: Where are we going? What is ahead? Is there anything beyond disintegration and the end of life?

These are the primal questions behind the art and idea of storytelling. "The imagination is indispensable to our existence and the speculations that reside in fiction, as presented in words, are the stimulant that facilitates that projection" (Adler 2015).

Adler acknowledges that there are those who will present passionate arguments for the superiority of the moving image over the written word. Audio and video messages are visually more appealing. As a society we are moving back to a deeper and refined oral tradition.

Still Adler believes that writing has its place. He argues for making "the preservation of the art of the written word a priority and finding the right balance between it and the moving image." There is authenticity in the written words. There is depth and persistence there. There imagination, creativity and commitment are combined. Human beings need more of it today! The growth and progress of our civilization demand more of written words, together with oral and other visual forms of communication and entertainment.

> "Writing and reading are the principal tools that inspire, create and empower our imagination without which we are bereft, muted and lesser. Anything that diminishes that power is the enemy of mankind."

35

Reading Rewrites Our Brain

Starting from writing, we move to reading, which also enhances our sense of the beautiful. One of the activities that make us healthier, smarter and more empathic is reading. The benefits are plenty, which is especially important in a distracted, smartphone age in many people don't learn to read. This not only endangers them socially and intellectually but cognitively handicaps them for life, writes Derek Beres, author of *Whole Motion: Training Your Brain and Body for Optimal Health*, in *BigThink*. He cites a 2009 study, according to which, reading creates new white matter in the brain, which improves system-wide communication.

White matter carries information between regions of grey matter, where any information is processed. Not only does reading increase white matter, but it also helps information be processed more efficiently.

Reading in one language has enormous benefits. Add a foreign language and not only do communication skills improve – you can talk to more people in wider circles – but the regions of your brain involved in spatial navigation and learning new information increase in size. Learning a new language also improves your overall memory, according to Beres (Beres 2017a).

So reading does, in fact, make us more intelligent. Research shows that reading not only helps with fluid intelligence, but with reading comprehension and emotional intelligence as well. You make smarter decisions about yourself and those around you.

All these benefits require reading, which leads "to the formation of a philosophy rather than the regurgitation of an agenda," normally found in reposts and online trolling. Recognizing the intentions of another human also plays a role in constructing a creative philosophy. Novels are especially well-suited for this task. A 2011 study found overlap in brain regions used to comprehend stories and networks dedicated to interactions with others.

Novels consume time and attention. While the benefits are worthwhile, even shorter bursts of prose exhibit profound neurological effects. Poetry elicits strong emotional responses in readers and, as one study shows, listeners. Heart rates, facial expressions and "movement of their skin and arm hairs" were measured while participants listened to poetry. Forty per cent ended up displaying visible goose bumps, while listening to music or watching movies.

Their neurological responses, however, seemed to be unique to poetry: Scans taken during the study showed that listening to the poems activated parts of participants' brains that, as other studies have shown, are not activated when listening to music or watching films.

These responses mostly occurred near the conclusion of a stanza and especially near the end of the poem. This fits in well with our inherent need for narrative: in the absence of a conclusion our brain automatically creates one, which, of course, leads to plenty of heartbreak and suffering when our speculations prove to be false. Instead, we should turn to more poetry since, "There is something fundamental to the poetic form that implies, creates and instils pleasure" (Beres 2017a).

In reading, paying attention really matters. Research at Stanford showed a neurological difference between reading for pleasure and focused reading, as if for a test. Blood flows to different neural areas depending on how reading is conducted. Like any skill we need to practice reading, regularly and constantly. Beres holds that "life would seem a bit less meaningful if we didn't share stories with one another." He adds: "While many mediums for transmitting narratives across space and time exist, I've found none as pleasurable as cracking open a new book and getting lost in a story. Something profound is always discovered along the way" (Beres 2017a).

Scanning headlines and retweeting is not reading. "Information gathering in under 140 characters is lazy. The benefits of contemplation through narrative offer another story" (Beres 2017a). We need to build a community that contemplates through shared narratives and reading. We need to read, write and engage. We need to reflect, critique and create. We need serious and sincere analysis leading to imagination. The patience, diligence and determination required for reading make us better!

Information gathering in under 140 characters is lazy. The benefits of contemplation through narrative offer another story". We need to build a community that contemplates through shared narratives and reading. We need to read, write and engage. We need to reflect, critique and create. We need serious and sincere analysis leading to imagination.

36

Music Enhances Empathy

Like writing and reading, music also makes us more aware of the beautiful. It deepens our sense of empathy. So we ask: How can music enhance empathy? People with higher empathy differ from others in the way their brains process music, according to a study by researchers at Southern Methodist University (SMU), Dallas and University of California, Los Angeles (UCLA) (Bergland 2018).

The researchers found that compared to low empathy people, those with higher empathy process familiar music with greater involvement of the reward system of the brain.

"High-empathy and low-empathy people share a lot in common when listening to music, including roughly equivalent involvement in the regions of the brain related to auditory, emotion and sensory-motor processing," said lead author Zachary Wallmark, an assistant professor in the SMU Meadows School of the Arts, according to *Psychology Today* (Bergland 2018).

Highly empathic people process familiar music with greater involvement of the brain's social circuitry, such as the areas activated when feeling empathy for others. They also seem to experience a greater degree of pleasure in listening, as indicated by increased activation of the reward system. "This may indicate that music is being perceived weakly as a kind of social entity, as an imagined or virtual human presence," Wallmark said.

The SMU-UCLA study is the first to find evidence supporting a neural account of the music-empathy connection. Also, it is among the first to use functional magnetic resonance imaging (fMRI) to explore how empathy affects the way we perceive music.

The new study indicates that, at least, music is more than artistic expression. "If music was not related to how we process the social world, then we likely would have seen no significant difference in the brain activation between high-empathy and low-empathy people," said Wallmark (Bergland 2018).

"This tells us that over and above appreciating music as high art, music is about humans interacting with other humans and trying to understand and communicate with each other," he added.

"But in our culture, we have a whole elaborate system of music education and music thinking that treats music as a sort of disembodied object of aesthetic contemplation," Wallmark said. "In contrast, the results of our study help explain how music connects us to others. This could have implications for how we understand the function of music in our world and possibly in our evolutionary past."

"The study shows … the power of empathy in modulating music perception, a phenomenon that reminds us of the original roots of the concept of empathy – 'feeling into' a piece of art," said senior author Marco Iacoboni, a neuroscientist at the UCLA Semel Institute for Neuroscience and Human Behavior (Bergland 2018).

Iacoboni said that the study also shows "the power of music in triggering the same complex social processes at work in the brain that are at play during human social interactions."

Further, the brain scans of higher empathy people in the study also recorded greater activation in medial and lateral areas of the prefrontal cortex that are responsible for processing the social world and in the temporoparietal junction, which is critical to analyzing and understanding others' behaviours and intentions.

Typically, those areas of the brain are activated when people are interacting with, or thinking about, other people. Observing their correlation with empathy during music listening might indicate that music to these listeners functions as a proxy for a human encounter.

Beyond analysis of the brain scans, the researchers also looked at purely behavioural data – answers to a survey asking the listeners to rate the music afterwards. Those data also indicated that higher empathy people were more passionate in their musical likes and dislikes, such as showing a stronger preference for unfamiliar music.

People who deeply grasp the pain or happiness of others also process music differently! Can we use this link between empathy and music to foster better artistic and social commitment? Today we need people who can empathise with the agony and pain as well as the joy and hope of the larger society? Perhaps we can all become musicians of joy and sadness of our own sisters and brothers and that of the sobbing earth.

People who deeply grasp the pain or happiness of others also process music differently! Can we use this link between empathy and music to foster better artistic and social commitment? Today we need people who can empathise with the agony and pain as well as the joy and hope of the larger society? Perhaps we can all become musicians of joy and sadness of our own sisters and brothers and that of the sobbing earth.

PART - X

Discovering the Meaning of me in the Cosmos

37

The Good Always Triumph

After reflecting on the beautiful dimensions of life, we focus here on the depth of ourselves and our values. In this depth, we can also feel traces of the Divine. First on reflect on the natural urge that truth (together with beauty) will have the final word.

In the final hours of 2015, Pope Francis encouraged humanity to hang on to recollections of good deeds, so that gestures of goodness can be seen triumphing over evil. Presiding over the final prayer service December 31, 2015 Thursday evening in St. Peter's Basilica, Rome, he wondered how people are sometimes driven by "insatiable thirst for power and by gratuitous violence."

In his brief homily, Francis said the outgoing year had been marked by many tragedies. There had been "violence, death, unspeakable suffering by so many innocent people, refugees forced to leaves their countries, men, women and children without homes, food or means of support" (Philip 2015).

But he said there had also been "so many great gestures of goodness" to help those in need, "even if they are not on television news programmes (because) good things don't make news". Francis added "These signs of love can't and mustn't be obscured by the tyranny of evil" and that good always triumphs. He urged the media to give more space to positive, inspirational stories to counterbalance the "preponderance of evil, violence and hate in the world" (Philip 2015).

In a similar vein, *Huffington Post* journalist Indrani Basu writes "These Stories We Covered In 2015 Highlight All That Is Right With The World." She agrees with the Pope that the past year has seen several controversies, human tragedies, terrorist strikes, grisly crimes, communal clashes and natural disasters. "It is easy to lose sight of the good things that happened when faced with a torrent of bad news. As many of these stories illustrate, it is sometimes at the darkest times that great things happen," she reminds us. Some such moments from 2015 that invites us to keep faith in humanity (Basu 2015).

For example, Prakash Rao had to give up his own education to support his family, but this tea seller from Odisha makes sure children around him go to school and get proper nutrition too. He plays the dual role of a *chaiwallah* and a teacher in Cuttack, where he educates approximately 70 children from class 1 to 3, following which he registers them in government schools.

Sadly, discriminating against those cooking our meals was not just subjected to those belonging to 'lower castes', but also to widowed women. But the simple act of one man helped overcome years of superstition in a district in Bihar. When a widowed woman was sacked from her job as a cook in the local government school the district magistrate Rahul Kumar decided to eat in public the meal prepared by her. His inspiring example helped her retain the job and won him deserved applause in the social media (Basu 2015).

A group of eight doctors working in one of the best city hospitals gave up their jobs to bring affordable health care to rural Chhattisgarh. These doctors charged nothing for their services, depending only on the funds from governmental and non-governmental agencies.

Even during the devastating floods in Chennai, there were many acts of human compassion. One poignant one is the story of a Hindu couple who have named their new-born after a Muslim who rescued them in the critical moments.

These are not merely anecdotal stories to deepen our faith in our humanity. Such actions and attitude, most of the time silently accomplished, form our core human nature and connect us to the best in ourselves and in the other. Every religion and culture, including our nation, hopes "Satyameva Jayate."

It is our religious responsibility to look at the evil directly and to experience its incurable harm. Then we need to explore the tremendous goodness in our human hearts and society. The good outweighs – not just will outweigh – the evil! We need to rediscover this common thread of goodness and beauty, even against the glamour of greed and selfishness.

It is our religious responsibility to look at the evil directly and to experience its incurable harm. Then we need to explore the tremendous goodness in our human hearts and society. The good outweighs – not just will outweigh – the evil! We need to rediscover this common thread of goodness and beauty, even against the glamour of greed and selfishness.

38

Encountering Persons

At the depth of our being is the desire to meet fellow-human beings as they are. We are challenged to look into their years and see their hearts, wherein dwells God. So, the challenge to encounter human persons in their difference and similarities.

How can we better encounter fellow human beings? Does the latest technology enable us to know ourselves deeper? Pope Francis hosted a special guest at the Vatican, Mark Zuckerberg, the founder of Facebook. It is reported that Zuckerberg and his wife, Priscilla Chan, spoke with Francis about "how to use communications technology to alleviate poverty, encourage a culture of encounter and to communicate a message of hope, especially to the most disadvantaged."

It's difficult to imagine two more different world leaders hanging out together, writes Emma Green is a senior associate editor at *The Atlantic.* Zuckerberg was raised in a Jewish home, identifies as an atheist and professes a profound respect for Buddhism. His social-media company claims to have a mission oriented toward creating social good, but in practice, it often leverages its immense influence over the way people use the internet "for profit and political power" (Green 2016). By his own description, the Facebook founder is interested in saving the world through technology.

Against that Pope Francis is aggressively anti-technology, in the sense that he actively warns against the belief that technological tools alone can be used to redeem or fix the world. There is quite a lot of evidence in his 2015 encyclical on the environment, *Laudato Si'*, along with his other writings, to suggest that he sees technological progress as possibly a dangerous goal. "Technology, which, linked to business interests, is presented as the only way of solving ... problems, in fact proves incapable of seeing the mysterious network of relations between things and so sometimes solves one problem only to create others," the pope wrote.

Francis sees the development of technological tools as directly connected to the search for profit; and this, he says, always damages human relationships. And the orientation toward profit, rather than bonds, "has made it easy to accept the idea of infinite or unlimited growth, which proves so attractive to economists, financiers and experts in technology."

"This indictment seems directed exactly at people like Zuckerberg, who drive and promote the total takeover of a socially networked world to extreme financial benefit," writes Green. But Francis's critique is not just about the moneymaking; he believes that "media," including the digital networks that dominate communication in many parts of the world, "stop people from learning how to live wisely, to think deeply and to love generously." When this happens, Francis writes, "the great sages of the past run the risk of going unheard amid the noise and distractions of an information overload" (Green 2016).

Francis, who spent time in the slums in Argentina and who urged the church leaders to "smell like the sheep," has critiqued what he sees as the abstraction of digital culture. Media can "shield us from direct contact with the pain, the fears and the joys of others and the complexity of their personal experiences," he wrote in *Laudato Si.* "For this reason, we should be concerned that, alongside the exciting possibilities offered by these media, a deep and melancholic dissatisfaction with interpersonal relations, or a harmful sense of isolation, can also arise" (*Laudato Si'* 47).

In this context the encounter between two persons with quite different mentality is noteworthy. Zuckerberg presented the Pope with a model of a futuristic Facebook drone, which is "symbolic of an ideology he and the Pope share" (Green 2016). He added: "We told him how much we admire his message of mercy and tenderness and how he's found new ways to communicate with people of every faith around the world."

"We also discussed the importance of connecting people, especially in parts of the world without internet access," Zuckerberg wrote. The greatest need today is to connect with people who think, live and behave quite different from us, by respecting their genuine differences. Only such a respectful acceptance of the other with their differences can lead us to enriching encounters.

Connections are critical. Relationship is life. We need to meet each other personally, intimately and intensely. Social network, to the extent it fosters such intimacy, is creative. It can also distract us from real communion and communication.

Connections are critical. Relationship is life. We need to meet each other personally, intimately and intensely. Social network, to the extent it fosters such intimacy, is creative. It can also distract us from real communion and communication.

39

Understanding Each Other

Encountering the other person, that we saw in the previous section, help us to understand the other at a deeper level. How do we understand and encounter people? But how can we be sure if our audiences understand what we're trying to convey? And better yet, how can we improve genuine understanding and facilitate better interaction?

Philadelphia's Drexel University biomedical engineers, in collaboration with New Jersey's Princeton University psychologists, are using a wearable brain-imaging device to see just how brains sync up when humans interact. It is one of many applications for this functional near-infrared spectroscopy (or fNIRS) system, which uses light to measure neural activity during real-life situations and can be worn like a headband (Drexel University 2017).

Published in *Scientific Reports* and reported *ScienceDaily*, this new study shows that the fNIRS device can successfully measure brain synchronization during a conversation. The technology can now be used to study everything from doctor-patient communication, to how people consume cable news.

"Being able to look at how multiple brains interact is an emerging context in social neuroscience," said Hasan Ayaz, PhD, an associate research professor in Drexel's School of Biomedical Engineering, Science and Health Systems, who led the research team. "We live in a social world where everybody is interacting. And we now have a tool that can give us richer information about the brain during everyday tasks – such as natural communication – that we could not receive in artificial lab settings or from single brain studies" (Drexel University 2017).

The current study is based on previous research from Uri Hasson, PhD, associate professor at Princeton University, who has used functional Magnetic Resonance Imaging (fMRI) to study the brain mechanisms underlying the production and comprehension of language. Hasson has found that a listener's brain activity mirrors the speaker's brain when he or she is telling story about a real-life experience. It is noted that higher coupling is associated with better understanding.

The Drexel researchers sought to investigate whether the portable fNIRS system could be a more effective approach to probe the brain-to-brain coupling question in natural settings.

For their study, a native English speaker and two native Turkish speakers told an unrehearsed, real-life story in their native language. Their stories were recorded and their brains were scanned using fNIRS. Fifteen English speakers then listened to the recording, in addition to a story that was recorded at a live storytelling event (Drexel University 2017).

The researchers targeted the prefrontal and parietal areas of the brain, which include cognitive and higher-order areas that are involved in a person's capacity to discern beliefs, desires and goals of others. They hypothesized that a listener's brain activity would correlate with the speaker's only when listening to a story they understood. A second objective of the study was to compare the fNIRS results with data from a similar study that had used fMRI, in order to compare the two methods.

They found that when the fNIRS measured the oxygenation and deoxygenation of blood cells in the test subject's brains, the listeners' brain activity matched only with the English speakers. These results also correlated with the previous fMRI study.

This new research supports fFNIRS as a viable future tool to study brain-to-brain coupling during social interaction. The system can be used to offer important information about how to better communicate in many different environments, including classrooms, business meetings, political rallies and doctors' offices (Drexel University 2017).

Banu Onaral, PhD, the H. H. Sun Professor in the School of Biomedical Engineering, Science and Health Systems say: "Now that we know fNIRS is a feasible tool, we are moving into an exciting era when we can know so much more about how the brain works as people engage in everyday tasks" (Drexel University 2017).

Studying how our brains interact with each other can lead to a better understanding among human beings. Today we need such deeper understanding both at the individual and collective domains, enriching our collective living. Without such a deeper understanding our fate is uncertain and survival questionable!

Studying how our brains interact with each other can lead to a better understanding among human beings. Today we need such deeper understanding both at the individual and collective domains, enriching our collective living. Without such a deeper understanding our fate is uncertain and survival questionable!

40

Face to Face

Encountering the other enables us to look at each other with compassion. To look at the eyes of the other and not to feel threatened. To be face to face with each other.

Science holds that our face we see in the mirror is the result of millions of years of evolution and reflects the most distinctive features that we use to identify and recognize each other, moulded by our need to eat, breath, see and communicate.

But how did the modern human face evolve to look the way it does? Eight of the top experts on the evolution of the human face, including Arizona State University's William Kimbel, collaborated on an article published this week in the journal *Nature Ecology & Evolution* to tell this four-million-year story. Kimbel is the director of the Institute of Human Origins and Virginia M. Ullman Professor of Natural History and the Environment in the School of Human Evolution and Social Change (Arizona State University 2019).

After our ancestors stood on two legs and began to walk upright, at least 4.5 million years ago, the skeletal framework of a bipedal creature was well formed. Limbs and digits became longer or shorter, but the functional architecture of bipedal locomotion had developed.

But the skull and teeth provide a rich library of changes that we can track over time, describing the history of the evolution of our species.

Prime factors in the changing structure of the face include a growing brain and adaptations to respiratory and energy demands, but most importantly, changes in the jaw, teeth and face responded to shifts in diet and feeding behaviour. We are, or we evolved to be, what we eat – literally!

Diet has played a large role in explaining evolutionary changes in facial shape. The earliest human ancestors ate tough plant foods that required large jaw muscles and cheek teeth to break down and their faces were correspondingly broad and deep, with massive muscle attachment areas.

As the environment changed to drier, less wooded conditions, especially in the last two million years, early Homo species began to routinely use tools to break down foods or cut meat. The jaws and teeth changed to meet a less demanding food source and the face became more delicate, with a flatter countenance (Arizona State University 2019).

Changes in the human face may not be due only to purely mechanical factors. The human face, after all, plays an important role in social interaction, emotion and communication. Some of these changes may be driven, in part, by social context. Our ancestors were challenged by the environment and increasingly impacted by culture and social factors. Over time, the ability to form diverse facial expressions likely enhanced nonverbal communication, reports *Science Daily.*

Large, protruding brow ridges are typical of some extinct species of our own genus, *Homo*, like *Homo erectus* and the *Neanderthals*. What function did these structures play in adaptive changes in the face? The African great apes also have strong brow ridges, which researchers suggest help to communicate dominance or aggression. It is probably safe to conclude that similar social functions influenced the facial form of our ancestors and extinct relatives. Along with large, sharp canine teeth, large brow ridges were lost along the evolutionary road to our own species, perhaps as we evolved to become less aggressive and more cooperative in social contexts, reports the study by Arizona State University, USA (Arizona State University 2019).

"We are a product of our past," says Kimbel. "Understanding the process by which we became human entitles us to look at our own anatomy with wonder and to ask what different parts of our anatomy tell us about the historical pathway to modernity" (Arizona State University 2019).

Our face, part of the process of evolution that has begun millions of years ago, make us truly unique. Can we look at the face of the other, respectfully and reverentially, so that we can see, as the Jewish philosopher, Emmanuel Levinas would say, the "trace of infinity (or Divine!) in the face of the other"? Can we contemplate the face of the Infinity in the trace of in our own face that we can glimpse only in the other – or in mirror?

Our face, part of the process of evolution that has begun millions of years ago, make us truly unique. Can we look at the face of the other, respectfully and reverentially, so that we can see, as the Jewish philosopher, Emmanuel Levinas would say, the "trace of infinity (or Divine!) in the face of the other"? Can we contemplate the face of the Infinity in the trace of in our own face that we can glimpse only in the other – or in mirror?

41

Understanding the World Better

Encountering humans help us to encounter the larger world and understand it better. We also refer to the paranormal world and the subconscious mind in this article.

Religious believers are more likely to have "a poorer understanding of the world and are more likely to believe objects like rocks and paper have human qualities," scientists say. Recently researchers compared believers in God or the paranormal to people with autism after finding they tend to struggle to understand the realities of the world around us.

Religious beliefs were linked with a weaker ability to understand physical and biological phenomenon such as volcanoes, flowers, rocks and wind without giving them human qualities, writes journalist Paul Ratner in *Big Think* (Ratner 2016).

The authors Marjaana Lindeman and Annika Svedholm-Häkkinen from University of Helsinki, who completed the research, claimed: "The more the participants believed in religious or other paranormal phenomena, the lower their intuitive physics skills, mechanical and mental rotation abilities, school grades in mathematics and physics and knowledge about physical and biological phenomena were… and the more they regarded inanimate targets as mental phenomena" (Ratner 2016).

The researchers said their findings suggest people's lack of understanding about the physical world means they apply their own, human characteristics to the whole universe, "resulting in belief in demons, gods and other supernatural phenomena". This confusion between mental and physical qualities "has [also] been recognised mainly among ancient people and small children", they added.

Further, the scientists compared religious believers to people with autism, saying both struggle to distinguish between the mental and the physical, although autistic people are at the opposite end of the spectrum because they often see the world as entirely physical and struggle to understand the mental state of others.

Ms Lindeman and Ms Svedholm-Häkkinen asked 258 Finnish people to report how much they agreed that "there exists an all-powerful, all-knowing, loving God" (Kentish 2016) and whether they believed in paranormal phenomena such as telepathy and visions of the future. They then matched their answers with a range of other factors, including exam results, survey answers and performances on different tests.

They also found that people who believe in God and the paranormal are more likely to be women and tend to base their actions on instinct rather than analytical thinking.

Kentish says that earlier studies have suggested religious people tend to have a lower IQ and are more likely to believe literally in what scientists called "bullshit statements" including phrases like "Earth wants water" and "Force knows its direction". However, they are also found to be happier and have greater life satisfaction than non-believers and are more generous and trustworthy (Kentish 2016).

Thus, the study concludes that scientifically minded people understand the world better. But a reply from a reader gives another nuance. The reader asserts that the "reason why most people still have religious or 'irrational' beliefs, instead of falling into line behind the 'pure and absolute truth' of science is that any discussion of human's place in the universe and why we came to be here in the first place, is regarded as an extraneous diversion" for science.

The reader further asks: Is it reasonable to expect that the man in the street will be content with being told, "Your life is pointless and you are destined by scientific fate to be a sterile, meaningless speck of stardust in an infinite vacuum of nothing, but be of good cheer: science will tell you how to power you automobile with pig droppings"? (Kentish 2016).

We need to understand that when it comes to the physical and biological world, science definitely helps us to understand the world better. But religion enables us to situate ourselves critically, creatively and meaningfully in our world? Is it not a deeper way of coping with reality? Can we reduce everything – including our emotions, existential anxieties and aspirations – to the scientific word?

42

What Really Matters in Life

After encountering fellow human beings and the world better, as we have attempted in the previous section, the important question remains: What is important and significant for us?

In a world that daily throws both curiosities and crises at us, it can be difficult to discern what is important. An unexpected event can render what matters today insignificant tomorrow. What really matters in our changing lives? How do you keep perspective? How do we really cherish now what matters most?

In order to find the answer, professional photographer, Nancy Hill turned to two groups – children under seven and adults over 70 – and posed this this question to them: What is important?

Children, according to Hill, have relatively little to clutter their lives and in their simplicity, they might be able to hone in on what really matters. "Adults with more than seven decades of experience would have deep insight into what is most worthy of attention," writes Hill in *YesMagazine*. Hill, "Three Things That Matter Most in Youth and Old Age by Nancy Hill — YES! Magazine" (Hill 2016).

She expected to find patterns in the answers of both these groups. In fact, what people left out of their list of important items was as telling as what they included. Interestingly, no one named prestige or individual success and hardly anyone mentioned money as the most important thing in life.

Another surprise was that we live among such remarkable people, yet few know their stories. Most of the time we forget that we live among such remarkable people, yet few know their stories.

Regarding people who are above seventy years old, why do we show such little appreciation for people beyond a certain age? Policy and decision makers rarely seek their advice. Their faces do not grace the cover of magazines.

She came away from this project with her own list of what is important. At the top of that list is the importance of connecting with others in general, but in particular with those who have lived long lives. Her advice to us is not let these people disappear quietly into their homes. He asks us to "draw them out, engage them in conversation and learn from them" (Hill 2016).

One of her respondents was Alex Panasenko, who was separated from his Russian family (which was living in Germany at the time) and sent to a German work camp when he was 10 years old. He was released a year later with no idea where his family was. He survived by selling things in the black market. As an adult, he taught Advanced Placement Science in a Berkeley, California, high school. He served in the Korean War. The three important things in his life: His wife Sally, his dog Lucy and going out! Six-year-old Nia has her family, her sister and her dog as the most important things in life.

Akhila Mudigonda, spent her childhood and most of her adulthood in India. She suffered a stroke several years ago, but she still makes clay sculptures of religious figures and animals. For her the most important things are spirituality (understanding "the deeper meaning in the ocean of Indian spiritual thought"), eternal optimism and education with development. For Payton, it is riding his bikes, playing with friends and swimming (Hill 2016).

What three things matter most to me? It is good to make a list for today. "It may also help me to go back to the time when I was seven years old, imagine my situation and make another list of what would have been the list of the three important things. Further, it will be good exercise to imagine myself reaching retirement and the age of seventy. Then I can write the three most important things for my 70-year-old self," writes another young person.

Keeping track of the three important things will help me to relativise my values and at the same time to hold on to what really matters in my changing and precious life. If we can look at things and people who really matters, we will lead lives that are more meaningful and enriching.

Keeping track of the three important things will help me to relativise my values and at the same time to hold on to what really matters in my changing and precious life. If we can look at things and people who really matters, we will lead lives that are more meaningful and enriching.

43

John Vattanky: Love and Logic

Finally, in our search to understand ourselves and the world two crucial things are love and logic. We dwell on the life of a great personality who has tried to combine both these aspects to lead a fruitful and productive life. Here we can encounter God as the basis and fullness of life.

One of the most eminent contemporary Indian Christian thinkers, Prof. John Vattanky SJ, has been a pioneer in making the classical Indian logic, Navya-Nyāya, popular to the contemporary world. A professional philosopher, he was inspired by late 12th-century Indian mathematician and philosopher Gangesha Upadhyaya. Throughout his philosophical search, he has constantly been seeking God. He found the fulfilment of his wish in the last days of his life in the person and spirituality of St. Ephrem the Syrian (306-373).

Throughout his life, he has been an earnest seeker: both philosophically and spiritually. He has also inspired countless people - both colleagues and students - in their pursuit of intellectual and spiritual fulfilment. So as a guide, mentor and inspiration, he has contributed significantly to Indian philosophy and Christian spirituality.

It is obvious that he has been the world authority on Navya-Nyāya. While in Pune, he had the most sought-after scholar, both nationally and internationally. To acknowledge Professor Vattanky's astounding contribution both to India and to Church, some of his colleagues and admirers have come together. While facilitating him respectfully and reverentially, we acknowledge our indebtedness to this generous personality.

It may be recalled that he returned from Pune to Kerala in June 2013. After more than a year on 30 December 2014, he had a stroke, which has left him paralysed. He is fully conscious but is totally dependent on others. We are happy that he has taken this situation gracefully and even with a sense of humour. His deep trust in God has been one of the factors that has kept him mentally agile.

So this book is a humble homage to our guru, mentor and guide. Through this book, we acknowledge Vattanky's contribution not only to the Indian philosophy and Indian Church but also at the personal level. He has personally touched and inspired us.

The title of the book, *Logic and Love: Reflecting on Professor John Vattanky's Contribution to Indian Philosophy and Spirituality* (Karimundackal and Pandikattu 2019) reflects Prof Vattanky total involvement in Navya-Nyāya (logic) through a deep spiritual devotion (love). The world authority he is on Navya-Nyāya, had no hesitation to surrender himself unconditionally to the God of Love thorough a spirituality and ethics that is world-affirming and intellectually vibrant.

This book, which we humbly offer to him, is divided into four parts, reflecting Vattanky's own philosophical vision and concerns. Each of these parts deals with both Indian and Western notions and categories. This reflects Vattanky's own eagerness to dialogue with Indian and Western traditions intellectually and affectively.

The first part deals with Logic and Nyāya, the field of Vattanky's own expertise. The next three article deals with the role of logic in contemporary science. The next part deals with the role and significance of hermeneutics or interpretation in our thinking and living. The final part deals with dharma and ethics, topics very dear to the heart of Prof. Vattanky and their relevance for contemporary society.

The world-authority of Nayva-nyaya logic challenges us through his life and work to relate logic to love; to mingle life with reason, to bring faith to our thinking and to make living and loving commitment to God by living in this world with critical thoughts. Can logic lead to love? Conversely, can love be purified by reason?

> The world-authority of Nayva-nyaya logic, Prof. Vattany challenges us through his life and work to relate logic to love; to mingle life with reason, to bring faith to our thinking and to make living and loving commitment to God by living in this world with critical thoughts. Can logic lead to love? Conversely, can love be purified by reason?

PART - VII
Empowering Through Storying

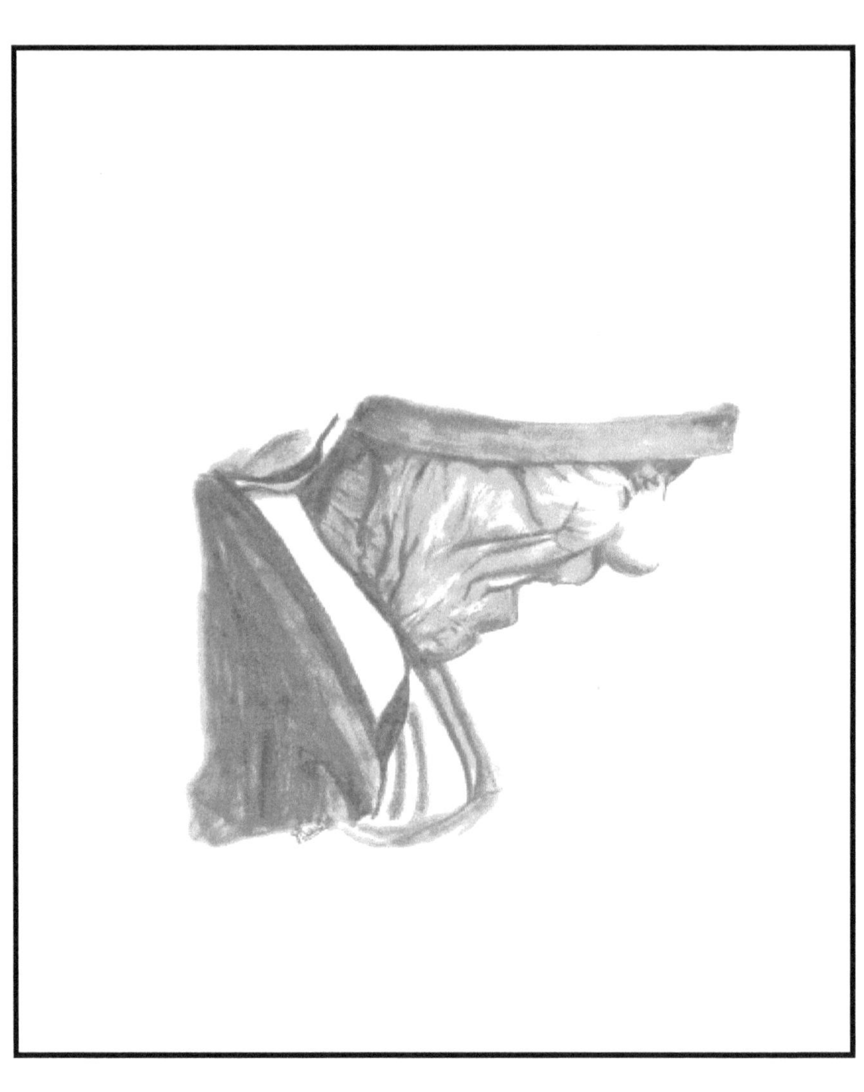

44

How Stories Can Liberate Us

After having explored the depth of our own lives, we shall try to see how we live the stories that we create for our own lives. The values of our lives, its goals and joys are intimately tied to the stories that we tell ourselves: stories of birth, death, God and of ourselves. First, we see how stories can liberate us, or conversely enslave us.

Sometimes we wonder if we are not doomed "to eternal indifference to the human beings who suffer" by our own callous attitude. Science offers us a modicum of hope on the subject. In recent years, one of the strongest findings is that storytelling can break through our indifference and foster empathy even for distant peoples who might otherwise seem alien to us. This more than anything else gives us the ability to empathize with those with whom we do not identify demographically or otherwise. "Stories hold our attention while feeding the strong urge to find meaningful patterns in human behavior," claims Rick Shenken (2016), author of *Political Animals: How Our Stone Age Brain Gets in the Way of Smart Politics.*

As scientists have now demonstrated in experiments, the brain is a natural pattern finder. It wants one and one to equal two. Mysterious may be the will of God, but here on Earth we expect behaviour to be explicable. Stories are designed to establish cause and effect and once we understand what motivates people, we can usually find a way to empathize with them, writes Shenkman in *The Huffington Post* (Lindley 2017).

Stories connect us to people in a way nothing else can. It is the reason politicians repeatedly tell stories on the campaign trail. Years ago, Harvard social scientist Howard Gardner set out to discover what extraordinarily successful leaders have in common. After reviewing the lives of 11 luminaries, from Margaret Thatcher to Martin Luther King, Jr., he concluded that their success depended to a remarkable extent on their ability to communicate a compelling story or, as he put it, "narratives that help individuals think about and feel who they are, where they come from and where they are headed." These stories, he found, "constitute the single most powerful weapon in the leader's literary arsenal" (Donbishopsam 2016).

When people are reduced to numbers – as were the civilian victims of airpower during the Korean War and as are the civilians who become "collateral damage" in airstrikes in Iraq, Syria and elsewhere – we don't feel their pain, nor do we automatically put ourselves in their shoes, which is by definition what you do when you are feeling empathic. We have the bomber pilot's syndrome (Donbishopsam 2016). We do not feel anything for the victims below. Since the pilot does not see or experience the pain of the victims, he is callous about it.

This is one reason why antiwar movements matter. They tell stories about the victims of war. It was striking in the Vietnam years, for instance, how many Americans came to care for, say, a small naked Vietnamese girl napalmed near her village, or so many other Vietnamese civilians who suffered under a rain of American bombs, rockets, napalm and artillery shells. The stories that the massive antiwar movement regularly told here about the distant world being decimated by the U.S. war machine created a powerful sense of empathy among many, including active-duty American soldiers and veterans of the war, for the plight of the Vietnamese (Lindley 2017).

Storytelling happens to be in every human's toolkit. We are all born storytellers and attentive listeners. Biology may incline us to turn a cold eye on the suffering of people we cannot see and don't know. Stories can liberate us from this deafness.

Our brains do not have to stay in the Stone Age. It can evolve and make ourselves more attentive to the sufferings of the unfortunate ones around us. Stories can change us and transform us if we start re-telling them. Creative and concise stories can be powerful weapons to wake us of our own spiritual and moral slumber. They enable us to listen to the cry of the individuals paying the price for our callous attitude and careless action.

Our brains can evolve and make ourselves more attentive to the sufferings of the unfortunate ones around us. Stories can change us and transform us if we start re-telling them. Creative and concise stories can be powerful weapons to wake us of our own spiritual and moral slumber. They enable us to listen to the cry of the individuals paying the price for our callous attitude and careless action.

45

Shallowing our Present and Hollowing Our Past

Stories connect us to the past and future. They make our geography (physical location) and history (temporal location) relevant and thus connect to our fellow human beings and to God. Let us reflect so on our rootedness and openness.

Maria Popova, founder of *Brainpickings*, recalls her arrival to USA as a teenage immigrant from Eastern Europe with $800 my parents had cobbled together to last her a year. She thought about how my life might have turned out if immigration policies and attitudes were then what they are now and about the generations of immigrants who have devoted their lives to making this country what it is (Popova 2018).

She thought about the great physicist and inventor Michael Pupin, after whom the physics building at Columbia University is named, reflecting on his own improbable path from immigrant to inventor after arriving in America as a penniless teenage boy from Serbia. She thought also about American Playwriter James Baldwin and American cultural anthropologist Margaret Mead challenging the problematic nature of the melting pot metaphor and philosopher political theorist Hannah Arendt contemplating the many layers of the immigrant plight for identity.

It seems to her that in a country so fundamentally shaped by immigrants, a societal sentiment so suddenly unwelcoming to them can only be the product of an absurd narrowing of perspective – an unthinking self-expatriation from history, a willful blindness to the cultural legacy of the past and an inability to take the telescopic perspective so vital to inhabiting the present with lucidity, integrity and a deep sense of connection to the whole of humanity.

Somewhere in this cascade of thought and feeling, she was reminded of a brief and beautiful reflection by physicist Freeman Dyson (b. December 15, 1923) from his magnificent epistolary memoir, Maker of Patterns: An Autobiography Through Letters.

Dyson writes in a letter from January 2, 1948, shortly after arriving in America as a twenty-four-year-old Englishman, having survived World War II to work on some of the most exciting scientific questions of the twentieth century: "Several of my friends are second-generation Americans, whose parents came over from Germany or Poland or Lithuania or some such place and I am always curious to ask them questions about their parents' histories in Europe and their reasons for emigrating and their emotional backgrounds. Always I have been amazed to find that the young people know practically nothing and apparently care little, about such matters. It is very strange when one thinks how much we have absorbed about the history and society to which our family belonged" (Popova 2018).

In a sentiment evocative of Hannah Arendt's insight into how demagogues and dictators use loneliness as a weapon of oppression, Dyson adds a wonderfully generous and optimistic counterpoint: "Not that I dislike the Americans on the whole; it is probably in the long run a good thing that they live so much in the present and the future and so little in the past. The fact that they are more alone in the world than average English people probably accounts for their great spontaneous friendliness. I had heard this friendliness attributed to the size of the country and to people's loneliness in space, but I think the loneliness in time is more important" (Popova 2018).

The "patterns of comparable beauty in the dance of electrons jumping around atoms" invariably replicate themselves in this autobiography told through letters, one that combines accounts of wanton arms development with the not-inconsiderable demands of raising six children. As we once again attempt to guide society toward a more hopeful future, these letters, with their re-enactment of what, at first, seems like a distant past, reveal invaluable truths about human nature.

Dyson holds that "severing our connection to the past shallows our present and hollows our history." Can we hold on to our roots and be open to the future, even if we must leave our cherished homelands and identities? Can we deal with the impact of loneliness mentally and spiritually? Can we respect the migrants who are forced out of their own homes for differing reasons, some of which are of our own making? Can we find our roots both in place (geography) and time (history)? Only then can we together walk beyond the shallow present (neighbours) and hollow past (history).

"Severing our connection to the past shallows our present and hollows our history." Can we hold on to our roots and be open to the future, even if we must leave our cherished homelands and identities? Can we deal with the impact of loneliness mentally and spiritually?

46

Channelling Anger to Tenderness

As we saw in the last section, stories enable us to find our roots. They can also help us to channel our anger to tenderness and foster positive values.

So the questions we ask in this article are: How can we channel our anger to tenderness? What can we learn from the Inuit way of life? Back in the 1960s, a Harvard graduate student made a landmark discovery about the nature of human anger. At age 34, Jean Briggs, American ethnographer, travelled above the Arctic Circle and lived out on the Tundra for 17 months. There were no roads, no heating systems, no grocery stores. Winter temperatures could easily dip below minus 40 degrees Fahrenheit. Briggs persuaded an Inuit family to "adopt" her and "try to keep her alive," as the anthropologist wrote in 1970 according to authors Michaeleen Doucleff and Jane Greenhalgh speaking in National Public Radio.

At the time, many Inuit families lived similar to the way their ancestors had for thousands of years. They built igloos in the winter and tents in the summer. "And we ate only what the animals provided, such as fish, seal and caribou," says Myna Ishulutak, a film producer and language teacher who lived a similar lifestyle as a young girl (Doucleff and Greenhalgh 2019).

Briggs quickly realized something remarkable was going on in these families: The adults had an extraordinary ability to control their anger. "They never acted in anger toward me, although they were angry with me an awful lot," Briggs told the Canadian Broadcasting Corp. in an interview.

For instance, one time someone knocked a boiling pot of tea across the igloo, damaging the ice floor. No one changed their expression. "Too bad," the offender said calmly and went to refill the teapot. Briggs, who died in 2016, wrote up her observations in her first book, *Never in Anger (Briggs 1981)*. But she was left with a lingering question: How do Inuit parents instill this ability in their children? How do Inuit take tantrum-prone toddlers and turn them into cool-headed adults?

Then in 1971, Briggs found a clue. She was walking on a stony beach in the Arctic when she saw a young mother playing with her toddler – a little boy about 2 years old. The mom picked up a pebble and said, "'Hit me! Go on. Hit me harder,'" Briggs remembered. The boy threw the rock at his mother and she exclaimed, "Oooww. That hurts!"

Briggs was completely confused. The mom seemed to be teaching the child the opposite of what parents want. And her actions seemed to contradict everything Briggs knew about Inuit culture. "I thought, 'What is going on here?' "Briggs said in the radio interview (Doucleff and Greenhalgh 2019).

It turns out, the mom was executing a powerful parenting tool to teach her child how to control his anger – and one of the most intriguing parenting strategies I have come across.

The moms in Inuit community refers to one golden rule: Do not shout or yell at small children. Traditional Inuit parenting is incredibly nurturing and tender. If you took all the parenting styles around the world and ranked them by their gentleness, the Inuit approach would likely rank near the top. (They even have a special kiss for babies, where you put your nose against the cheek and sniff the skin.)

The culture views scolding – or even speaking to children in an angry voice – as inappropriate, says Lisa Ipeelie, a radio producer and mom who grew up with 12 siblings. "When they're little, it doesn't help to raise your voice," she says. "It will just make your own heart rate go up."

Even if the child hits you or bites you, there is no raising your voice? "No," Ipeelie says with a giggle that seems to emphasize how silly my question is. "With little kids, you often think they're pushing your buttons, but that's not what's going on. They're upset about something and you have to figure out what it is."

Traditionally, the Inuit saw yelling at a small child as demeaning. It is as if the adult is having a tantrum; it's basically stooping to the level of the child, Briggs documented. Elders I spoke with say intense colonization over the past century is damaging these traditions. And, so, the community is working hard to keep the parenting approach intact (Doucleff and Greenhalgh 2019).

Can we learn from the original Inuit community to raise children in freedom and joy? In playful spontaneity? And also, to free ourselves from anger and violence? Can we create a community where violence is fully channelized and anger is transformed? The world needs it badly!

Can we learn from the original Inuit community to raise children in freedom and joy? In playful spontaneity? And to free ourselves from anger and violence? Can we create a community where violence is fully channelized and anger is transformed? The world needs it badly.

47

Disciplining through Fun and Stories

Just like channeling our anger, stories also help us to discipline ourselves and others. Stories can truly shape the way we think, talk and behave!

When a child in the camp acted in anger — hit someone or had a tantrum — there was no punishment among the Inuits. Instead, the parents waited for the child to calm down and then, in a peaceful moment, did something that Shakespeare would understand all too well: They put on a drama, as Shakespeare would say: "The play's the thing wherein I'll catch the conscience of the king."

"The idea is to give the child experiences that will lead the child to develop rational thinking," Jean Briggs, American-born **anthropologist**, ethnographer, said. In general, the parent would act out what happened when the child misbehaved, including the real-life consequences of that behaviour.

The parent always had a playful, fun tone. And typically, the performance starts with a question, tempting the child to misbehave.

For example, if the child is hitting others, the mom may start a drama by asking: "Why don't you hit me?" Then the child must think: "What should I do?" If the child takes the bait and hits the mom, she does not scold or yell but instead acts out the consequences. "Ow, that hurts!" she might exclaim.

The mom continues to emphasise the consequences by asking a follow-up question. For example: "Don't you like me?" or "Are you a baby?" She is getting across the idea that hitting hurts people's feelings and "big girls" wouldn't hit. But, again, all questions are asked with a hint of playfulness (Doucleff and Greenhalgh 2019).

The parent repeats the drama from time to time until the child stops hitting the mom during the dramas and the misbehaviour ends. Ishulutak says these dramas teach children not to be provoked easily. "They teach you to be strong emotionally," she says, "to not take everything so seriously or to be scared of teasing."

Psychologist Peggy Miller, at the University of Illinois, agrees: "When you're little, you learn that people will provoke you and these dramas teach you to think and maintain some equilibrium."

In other words, the dramas offer kids a chance to *practice* controlling their anger, Miller says, during times when they are not actually angry. This practice is likely critical for children learning to control their anger. Because here is the thing about anger: Once someone is already angry, it is not easy for that person to squelch it — even for adults.

"When you try to control or change your emotions in the moment, that's a really hard thing to do," says Lisa Feldman Barrett, a psychologist at Northeastern University who studies how emotions work.

But if you *practice* having a different response or a different emotion at times when you are not angry, you'll have a better chance of managing your anger in those hot-button moments, Feldman Barrett says.

"That practice is essentially helping to rewire your brain to be able to make a different emotion [besides anger] much more easily," she says (Doucleff and Greenhalgh 2019). This emotional practice maybe even more important for children, says psychologist Markham, because kids' brains are still developing the circuitry needed for self-control.

"Children have all kinds of big emotions," she says. "They don't have much prefrontal cortex yet. So, what we do in responding to our child's emotions shapes their brain."

Markham recommends an approach close to that used by Inuit parents. When the kid misbehaves, she suggests, wait until everyone is calm. Then in a peaceful moment, go over what happened with the child. You can simply tell them the story about what occurred or use two stuffed animals to act it out. "Those approaches develop self-control," Markham hold.

Further, be sure to keep it fun. Many parents overlook play as a tool for discipline, Markham says. But fantasy play offers oodles of opportunities to teach children proper behaviour.

"Play is their work," Markham says. "That's how they learn about the world and about their experiences." This seems to be something the Inuit have known for hundreds, perhaps even, thousands of years. That is something the larger community can learn from them.

> When the kid misbehaves wait until everyone is calm. Then in a peaceful moment, go over what happened with the child. You can simply tell them the story about what occurred or use two stuffed animals to act it out. "Those approaches develop self-control!"

48

The Common Story of God

Finally, in this section on God, we can ask about our own stories of God. God who is present everywhere can be made more palpable through the stories that we narrate to ourselves.

Academy Award winner Morgan Freeman has played God in two feature films "Bruce Almighty" (2003) and "Evan Almighty" (2007). He has been up close and personal with God as a character in films, but his own experience of the divine is more nuanced than his playful portrayals might suggest. (Blumberg 2017)

Exploring questions about faith and the Almighty in *The National Geographic* show "The Story of God with Morgan Freeman," Freeman goes 20 cities in seven countries, investigating religious concepts that have intrigued philosophers for centuries.

He explores the meaning of life, God and many big questions in between to understand how religion has evolved and shaped society. A different divine subject is covered in each hourlong episode, titles of which include "Creation," "The Devil Inside," "Afterlife," "Apocalypse," and "Who Is God?" Travelling to different religious sites like Jerusalem's Wailing Wall, India's Bodhi Tree, Mayan temples in Guatemala and the pyramids of Egypt, he immerses himself in religious experiences and rituals. "In some places I found answers and others led to more questions.

The constant through it all is that we're all looking to be part of something bigger than us. If there's one thing I've learned, it's that we certainly are," Freeman says (Blumberg 2017).

The first season aired in the spring of 2016 and became *National Geographic*'s most-watched series of all time. "We're dealing with esoterica here, things that are more internal than external. So, there are always going to be more questions," Freeman claims. "It's one of those situations where the more you delve into it, the deeper it gets."

The second season features just three episodes exploring three fundamental religious themes. The first episode explores the concept of the "chosen one" - people who have been singled out throughout history for purportedly having direct access to the divine. Next, the show explores "heaven and hell," with a look at how people's beliefs about the afterlife influence their actions in this life. The final episode dives into the age-old question of whether there's "proof of God," and the subtle ways people of faith find look for it.

Freeman is an executive producer on the show, along with Lori McCreary and James Younger of Revelations Entertainment, which Freeman and McCreary co-founded. "Doing this series makes you realize, whatever your belief is, how important religion is to the structure of our daily lives," Younger told *HuffPost*, reports Antonia Blumberg, its associate religious editor (Blumberg 2017).

The Story of God" isn't a show about condemning faith's blind spots. It rarely even pits religions against one another, even when their different beliefs on a topic could fill an entire series. Instead, the show seeks to find common ground among faiths, which the producers acknowledged can be a novel concept in the world today.

"It's encouraging to see that so many varying belief systems have such a commitment to good deeds and being of service to their communities," McCreary said. Sharing that message of commonality is exactly what drove them to make the show, Younger said. "The events that happened around the world … in the last few months only make it more important that we do this kind of work, that we look for what we have in common with a person who appears to be different from us," he told *HuffPost*.

Taking a philosophical approach Freeman, holds that "The Story of God" shows something essential about religion itself. Religion is not the opiate of the masses. It is "more like the glue that holds societies together and religion in its very nature gives hope. I don't think it would exist in such a wide aspect if that were not the truth of it" (Blumberg 2017).

> "The Story of God" shows something essential about religion itself. Religion is not the opiate of the masses. It is "more like the glue that holds societies together and religion in its very nature gives hope. I don't think it would exist in such a wide aspect if that was not the truth of it"

PART - VIII

Being Attentive to the Society

49

Educating for a Better Society

After reflecting on the role of stories in shaping the attitude of society, in this section we dwell on the larger concerns of the society. How does a society maintain itself and be of service to its individual members? One of the ways is by imparting good education, as we see in this section.

On 24 January 2019, UN observed its very first International Day for Education. The event was held at the United Nations Headquarter and was sponsored and hosted by the Mission of Nigeria to the UN and co-sponsored by the Permanent Missions of Ireland, Singapore, Qatar, Norway and UNESCO.

The proposal was conceptualised and mooted by Christo Thomas, the Founder Chairman of Collegiate Congress, a student advocacy organisation which is a consortium of elected student leaders of universitics and colleges in New York (Khaira 2019).

Born in Kerala, Thomas is the son of Kerala lawyer-politician KJ Thomas. He studied at Kendriya Vidyalaya in Kannur's Keltron Nagar and has a bachelor's degree in political science and is pursuing his second master's in international Affairs.

The Collegiate Congress is an NGO associated with the United Nations Department of Public Information designed and proposed the resolution for the day. It was then moved at the UN by the Nigerian mission and co-sponsored by 58 member states, writes Rachna Khaira in *HuffPost, India*.

"It would have been great if India, known for its ancient scholars and scientists, had sponsored my resolution. Though I had discussions with the UN Missions of India and US, it was Nigeria who finally advocated the cause to celebrate the role of education for peace and development," said Thomas while speaking with *HuffPost India* over the phone from New York (Khaira 2019).

The idea of observing an International Day for Education came to Thomas while working on the first academic programme for United Nations Institute for Training and Research (UNITAR), the principal body of the UN that provides training to diplomats.

"While UN observes many international days, it did not have any assigned day for education, even though the UN Declaration of Human Rights clearly mentions Right to Education and quality education is the fourth Sustainable Development Goal. So, we as a UN affiliate organisation proposed the day," said Thomas (Khaira 2019).

He drafted the resolution with the help of senior UN Diplomats including Narinder Kakar, a permanent observer who had also served with the UN Development Programme for decades, Yuriy Sergeyev, former Ukrainian,ambassador, Frederick Bijou, former diplomat of Costa Rica and other member state representatives. The draft was then sent to over 40 countries, including India and US, writes Khaira (2019).

While India liked the resolution, it was too busy to sponsor it at the UN. "I reached out to India during the UN General Assembly session, which is the peak time for every member state, especially missions such as India who handle many issues in the UN. However, I am happy to see that they did co-sponsor it," Thomas said.

24 January was chosen as the day for the significance it held for the UN for its role in peace and development. "In 1946, UN had adopted its very first resolution on the establishment of a commission to deal with the problem raised by the discovery of atomic energy," said Thomas. On 3rd December 2018, the United Nations General Assembly unanimously adopted the resolution proclaiming 24th January as the International Day of Education.

Thomas said that adoption of the resolution by UN has "demonstrated the unwavering political will to support transformative actions for inclusive, equitable and quality education for all" (Khaira 2019). A day before on 23rd January 2019, New York became the first state in the world to adopt the resolution to acknowledge the UN International Day of Education.

"We have already started a global campaign for our new initiative befitting the importance of education, focused on two interrelated goals which include the global implementation of the International day of Education and promoting and supporting the UN Sustainable development Goals. This is a global initiative which will be unveiled mid this year," said Thomas.

Education enables, enhances, both the individual and society. It can foster a better and egalitarian society. But we must also acknowledge that sometimes education itself can become a means for continued oppression. Like knowledge, education provides power, which may, at times, be misused.

> Education enables, enhances, both the individual and society. It can foster a better and egalitarian society. But we must also acknowledge that sometimes education itself can become a means for continued oppression. Like knowledge, education provides power, which may, at times, be misused.

50

From One Generation to Another

Connected to the larger interests of the society, we see in this section how a society transmits its values, vision and other features. How are we related to our past generations? How are the characteristics passed on from generation to generation? How is information inherited?

We know traditionally that genes play a dominant role in transmitting characteristics from parent to children. Biological science today is convinced that we inherit more than just genes. Epigenetics are stable heritable traits (or "phenotypes") that cannot be explained by changes in DNA sequence.

Epigenetic mechanisms modulated by environmental cues such as diet, disease or our lifestyle take a major role in regulating the DNA by switching genes on and off. It has been long debated if epigenetic modifications accumulated throughout the entire life can cross the border of generations and be inherited to children or even grandchildren. Now researchers from the Max Planck Institute of Immunobiology and Epigenetics in Freiburg, Germany, show robust evidence that the inherited epigenetic instructions contribute in regulating gene expression in the offspring, reports *ScienceDaily* (Max-Planck-Gesellschaft 2017).

Moreover, the new insights of Nicola Iovino describe for the first-time biological consequences of this inherited information. The study proves that a mother's epigenetic memory is essential for the development and survival of the new generation.

In the human body, we find more than 250 different cell types. They all contain the same DNA bases in the same order; however, liver or nerve cells look very different and have different skills. What makes the difference is the process epigenetics. Epigenetic modifications label specific regions of the DNA to attract or keep away proteins that activate genes. Thus, these modifications create, step by step, the typical patterns of active and inactive DNA sequences for each cell type. Further, epigenetic marks can also change throughout our life and in response to our environment or lifestyle. For example, smoking changes the epigenetic makeup of lung cells, eventually leading to cancer.

Earlier it was thought that these epigenetic modifications are not passed on to the next generation. Scientists assumed that epigenetic memory is entirely cleared during the development of sperms and egg cells. Now they believe that the modifications are somehow transmitted. "We saw indications of intergenerational inheritance of epigenetic information since the rise of the epigenetics in the early nineties. For instance, epidemiological studies revealed a striking correlation between the food supply of grandfathers and an increased risk of diabetes and cardiovascular disease in their grandchildren," says Nicola Iovino, corresponding author (Max-Planck-Gesellschaft 2017).

Using fruit flies, the researchers found that modifications DNA in the mother's egg cells were still present in the embryo after fertilization, even though other epigenetic marks are erased. "This indicates that the mother passes on her epigenetic marks to her offspring. But we were also interested, if those marks are doing something important in the embryo," asserts Fides Zenk, first author of the study.

This study is an important step forward and clearly shows the biological consequences of inherited epigenetic information. Not only by providing evidence that epigenetic modifications in flies can be transmitted down through generations, but moreover by revealing that epigenetic marks transmitted from the mother are a fine-tuned mechanism to control gene activation during the complex process of early development of embryo.

"Our study indicates that we inherit more than just genes from our parents. It seems to be that we also get a fine-tuned as well as important gene regulation machinery that can be influenced by our environment and lifestyle. These insights can provide new ground for the observation that at least in some cases acquired environmental adaptations can be passed over the germline to our offspring," explains Nicola Iovino (Max-Planck-Gesellschaft 2017).

The traditional view that characteristics are passed on through genetic transmission needs to be revisited in the light of this experiment. This indicates that there is still so much to be investigated and known about our human body. We are much more interconnected or interlinked than we know. We are indebted to our past generations, much more than we imagine! We are truly part of the past and pass our knowledge and traits to our progeny.

We are much more interconnected or interlinked than we know. We are indebted to our past generations, much more than we imagine! We are truly part of the past and pass our knowledge and traits to our progeny.

51

The India of Our Dreams

In the coming two sections, we reflect on India as a living society and see how we can pay attention to India's rich heritage and contemporary vibrancy, both financially and spiritually. Here we see how India can project as a world leader of ideas: ideas of non-violence, democracy and freedom.

The speech "I have a dream," that Martin Luther King Jr delivered on 28th August 1963, was defining moment in the American Civil Rights movement, laying out his dream for a racially reconciled nation.

On 6th May 2016, Pope Francis delivered his own "I have a dream" address, in this case dedicated to Europe, calling the continent to undergo a "memory transfusion" to avoid the mistakes of the past and to pursue a future based on "economic justice, openness to newcomers, respect for life in all its stages and dialogue with everyone" (Martín 2016).

"I dream of a Europe that is young, still capable of being a mother: a mother who has life because she respects life and offers hope for life," Francis said, as he was accepting the prestigious Charlemagne Prize, given yearly to persons who have contributed to European unity.

The Pope added that "with hope and without vain nostalgia, like a son who rediscovers in Mother Europe his roots of life and faith," he dreams of a new "European humanism," involving "a constant work of humanization" and calls for "memory, courage, [and] a sound and humane utopian vision" (Martín 2016).

His dream for Europe, the Pontiff added, is of a continent that cares for children, one that helps the poor and newcomers "seeking acceptance because they have lost everything and need shelter."

He further dreams of a Europe where being a migrant is "not a crime, but a summons to greater commitment on behalf of the dignity of every human being."

His dream for Europe also includes fostering a love for honesty, beauty and simple life among the young. "I dream of a Europe that promotes and protects the rights of everyone, without neglecting its duties towards all" (Martín 2016).

Francis ended his address saying that he dreams "of a Europe of which it will not be said that its commitment to human rights was its last utopia."

"What has happened to you, Europe, the home of poets, philosophers, artists, musicians and men and women of letters?" he asked. "What has happened to you, Europe, the mother of peoples and nations, the mother of great men and women who upheld and even sacrificed their lives for, the dignity of their brothers and sisters?"

Francis also listed three "capacities" with which Europe would be able to create a "new European humanism," that would lead to his dreamed version of Europe: The capacity to integrate, the capacity for dialogue and the capacity to generate.

An integrated version of the European people, he said, would rediscover its soul, "born of the encounter of civilizations and peoples." The second capacity Europe should have, according to Francis, is that of dialogue, saying that peace would only be lasting in the measure "that we arm our children with the weapons of dialogue, that we teach them to fight the good fight of encounter and negotiation" (Martín 2016).

Lastly, the capacity to generate, with dialogue and openness to others, since "no one can remain a mere onlooker or bystander" in building an integrated and reconciled society.

Similar to the dream for Europe, can we share a dream for all the Indians, where we can draw from our inner wisdom and create a society that is egalitarian, free and respectful of each other? Can we draw from our spiritual depth and create a society of equals? Can Indians, with their natural diversity, show the world the beauty and depth of living together as brothers and sisters? Can we collectively foster India's capacity to integrate, the capacity for dialogue and the capacity to generate? Can we expect visionaries and leaders who will unify our country and making it a place of peace, prosperity and hospitality for all, as the freedom fighters dreamt? As Tagore sang?

Can we collectively foster India's capacity to integrate, the capacity for dialogue and the capacity to generate? Can we expect visionaries and leaders who will unify our country and making it a place of peace, prosperity and hospitality for all, as the freedom fighters dreamt?

52

The Dangers of Majoritarianism and Fundamentalism

"Science explains and religion gives meaning. Atheists have really struggled to do this on a communal level. Atheism has been trying to give meaning, but not successfully. Most atheist philosophies have turned into very violent nationalisms and this is yet another example of a story – albeit a secular one," claims Neil MacGregor, former director of the National Gallery, London and British Museum (Kohli 2018).

He elaborates: "In the former Soviet Union, communism became a religion and the teachings of Lenin and Marx took the place of the Holy Scripture. We haven't therefore seen an atheist state, although we have got various surrogates. And while individuals can be atheist in their own capacity, it is extremely difficult to carry this forward on a community level" (Kohli 2018).

The Indian situation is characterised by multiple narratives of religion that work for all of society. The Indian model strikes him as it has long struck Europeans as an example of multiple narratives. "It is why what is happening in India is so important for the world now. What has always been fascinating for Europeans is that from Ashoka to Akbar to Ambedkar and the Constitution, India has always understood that religion is an important part of the public life of the citizens. The state acknowledges that public role of religion and is at equidistance from all of them and that is Indian secularism," writes MacGregor, the author of *Living with the Gods* (MacGregor 2019).

The European tradition was completely different and there was one religion for the state and the ruler imposed it. It was unthinkable to have different religions as it would mean civil war and the state would split. Later, when European secularism emerged, it was a different secularism than in India. European secularism was clearly hostile towards religion and denied it a public role. The wisdom of the Indian model recognized that both politics and religion were about the same thing. The question being asked today is how people of different religions will live together (Kohli 2018). We are looking at India with concern and interest to see if the longstanding religious traditions of India are robust enough to negotiate the particular questions of today.

His take on the rise of majoritarianism and religious fundamentalism in India today is clear. Many thinkers have argued that what is happening is that European traditions of single religion nationalism, literal truths and Semitic monotheisms, which are alien to India are being introduced here. The European culture emerges from different contents and they are our historical inheritance.

Those problems and approaches are being introduced into India and it is a tension between a long traditional Indian way of thinking and exclusive habits of thought which are very characteristic of European thought and monotheism. It is this which leads to majoritarianism and religious fundamentalism, both of which are alien to India (Kohli 2018).

India has a rich tradition of "living with many gods" and with other diverse traditions. We will be losing this diversity, versatility, inventiveness and resourcefulness if we take up either majoritarianism or fundamentalism.

Being flexible, creative and versatile, India can create a future that is inclusive, diverse and respectful of others!

> India has a rich tradition of "living with many gods" and with other diverse traditions. We will be losing this diversity, versatility, inventiveness and resourcefulness if we take up either majoritarianism or fundamentalism. Being flexible, creative and versatile, India can create a future that is inclusive, diverse and respectful of others!

53

Beyond Entertainment: Relation between Faith and Culture

In searching for the identity of a nation (like India) or a religion, we cannot expect instant answers and immediate gratification. So we look at the larger impact of our faith or vision on our culture or society.

Today science is enjoying a much-needed moment in the popular cultural zeitgeist, as indicated by "March for Science" held in April 2017 and the popular TV show "*Bill Nye* Saves the World," by *Bill Nye, nicknamed* "the *Science* Guy."

Writing in *The Washington Post*, journalist Tyler Huckabee, holds that entertainment science is "in danger of the same pratfalls that have hamstrung another subculture with which it has more in common than its stewards might care to admit: the religious one" (Huckabee 2017).

He adds that religious entertainment could teach science a thing or two about the danger of pandering to pop culture. "Both science and faith try to use pop culture to get you to buy into a certain set of beliefs without boring you out of your skull. Both can safely assume a fair number of sceptics in their audiences and both are trying to convince you that - contrary to what you may have heard - the subject in question is both cool and relevant," writes Huckabee.

Coming to religion: In the '90s American televangelists tried to be cool and was initially successful. Today it has faded as it became increasingly clear that wherever else faith's natural habitat may be, it's not in the entertainment industry. "The whiz-bang pyrotechnics and giddy razzle-dazzle of mainstream pop culture simply don't lend themselves to faith, which thrives best in contemplation and reflection," Huckabee asserts (2017).

Likewise, science thrives on serious study and sustained commitment. As Carl Sagan reminds us, science is "a way of thinking much more than it is a body of knowledge." The danger with scientists like Nye and the well-known American astrophysicist Neil deGrasse Tyson pandering to the entertainment industry is that it often becomes reduced to generating headlines.

This is again unfortunate, says Huckabee, because, Tyson is a man of obvious intelligence and charm and his "Cosmos" reboot was outstanding. "There is no reason that such a naturally gifted communicator should waste his considerable talents on being the fun police for a superhero space romp. Doing so degrades his scientific brilliance to the same realm as the worst elements of the Christian subculture: turning a fascinating, mind-expanding tool for understanding reality into nothing more than a wet blanket," opines Huckabee (2017).

That, too, is reminiscent of some of the evangelical subculture at its most patronizing and imposing attitude. Faith and culture will always necessarily be in conversation, but not in a cheap and entertaining manner.

Science, like religion, provides a profoundly beautiful prism through which to help interpret the world. It is organized knowledge that, in its truest essence, uses what we know about the universe to help us grasp at those things that we do not. Unfortunately, dangerous, anti-intellectual bile about the "myth" of climate change and the "danger" of vaccines is being thrown around causally. Some solid science would go a long way toward fixing such disquieting trends.

In such dark times, it's easy to take any tiny win as progress, even something as dubious as a few extra retweets. The temptation to cater to the social media masses is understandably huge. But it may not serve the good of either science or religion.

But we need only look so far as a religion to see just where such tricks will take you. "The infantilization of religious discourse has elevated its worst elements, making heroes of people not fit to clean the boots of the likes of Martin Luther King Jr" (Huckabee 2017) or Mahatma Gandhi.

For all its mainstream embarrassments, rigorous, insightful conversations around religion are happening, albeit in smaller pockets, away from the spotlight. Science, obviously, continues to thrive in institutions of higher learning. This demands serious, dedicated commitment which may not provide us with instant satisfaction and popular acclaim. But such religion and science can speak with seriousness and depth. With rigour and vigour! Therein lies the future of committed religions, genuine sciences and a more humane world.

Both religion and science demand serious, dedicated commitment which may not provide us with instant satisfaction and popular acclaim. But such religion and science can speak with seriousness and depth. With rigour and vigour! Therein lies the future of committed religions, genuine sciences and a more humane world.

54

Magic and Society

Intricately connected with the society is magic, seen not as entertainment but as a way of understanding society better. How does magic contribute to understanding a society better?

What is magic? How is it connected to the unknown and unknowable? What does magic say about our brain? The magician picks up a coin, conceals it in his hand and, after a magical gesture, it mysteriously disappears, only to reappear from behind your ear. As you watch this performance, you fully understand that objects cannot simply materialise from thin air, yet this is exactly what you have just experienced. Conjuring is one of the oldest forms of entertainment and throughout history, tricksters have amazed audiences by performing illusions of the impossible.

The art of magic has never lost its appeal and even in our modern lives, which are dominated by science and technology, we are still captivated by experiencing things we believe to be impossible. This universal appeal can be traced back to a deep-rooted psychological drive to explore things we do not understand. Indeed, from an early age, infants are captivated by events that confound their understanding of the world and the same is true for adults. Most people simply think of magic as just another form of entertainment, but the ancient art of conjuring is now helping scientists uncover some of the mysteries of the human mind, writes Gustav Kuhn in *The Guardian*. Kuhn is the director of the MAGIC laboratory (Mind, Attention and General Illusory Cognition), Goldsmiths University of London and spends most of his time studying human cognition. Rather than performing magic to entertain people, I study magic in the lab (Kuhn 2019).

Magic deals with some of the most fundamental psychological and philosophical questions. What do you believe to be possible? What is consciousness? How much control do you have over your thoughts and your actions? And yet, until recently, the art of magic has received little scientific attention.

For most magicians, this link between magic and psychology is obvious. Magic relies on powerful psychological illusions and magicians create their tricks by exploiting gaps and errors in our conscious experience. For example, magicians use misdirection to manipulate what you attend to and this allows them to control what you see – and what you miss.

Gustav Kuhn (2019), the author of *Experiencing the Impossible: The Science of Magic,* used eye-tracking equipment to investigate how magicians misdirect people's attention. We developed fun experiments in which we used the tracker to measure people's eye movements while they watched me performing simple tricks. The results were astonishing – the misdirection was remarkably effective at manipulating people's conscious experiences. It was also the first time we had scientific data that helped us understand how misdirection works and we were surprised that people often failed to see things that were right in front of their eyes. The misdirection was so effective that some people were looking at an object, yet they simply did not see it. We soon realised magic could provide a useful tool to study visual attention (Kuhn 2019).

Our scientific approach is based on the following logic: magicians have spent hundreds of years developing the art of deception and by doing so they have discovered powerful tricks that capitalise on cognitive errors. Scientists regularly study cognitive errors, often by looking at psychological impairments caused by brain damage.

Magicians are not concerned with understanding the anatomy of the brain, but their experience in tricking people has helped them identify profound errors in cognition. Indeed, most magic tricks rely on exploiting surprising and powerful cognitive errors and magicians have informally learned to understand psychological principles that push our cognitive processes to a breaking point. By understanding these conjuring techniques and their underlying cognitive mechanisms, we can then gain valuable knowledge of how the mind works.

Much of our work on misdirection reveals that the gaps in our conscious experience are more prominent than most of us had assumed. As you look at your surroundings, you experience the world as a rich and complete sensory experience. However, our research on misdirection illustrates that this conscious experience is a powerful illusion. Our accurate perception is full of gaps and holes and much more removed from reality than most of us imagine. Kuhn spent much of his time studying these types of illusions and even though he knew his brain is being tricked, still struggle to appreciate just how little he is truly conscious of (Kuhn 2019). It is a very compelling illusion and one that is very difficult to break.

This research on misdirection has important real-world implications. It is often important to accurately judge our own cognitive abilities and misjudgments can have fatal consequences. For example, most people underestimate the extent to which their attention is misdirected by a phone call. Research has shown that talking even on a hands-free phone has the same detrimental impact on your driving as being over the drink-drive limit. However, since we overestimate our own abilities, we do not notice the effect this technological misdirection has on our performance.

Research on magic highlights that we are not only wrong about the amount we see, but also about the extent to which we can trust the things we see and remember. As we are learning more about the mind, it has become apparent that most of our experiences are an illusion.

The psychological mechanism that underpins forcing techniques that the magician imposes on the audience and the ease by which we can covertly manipulate people's decisions is intriguing. Most importantly these findings illustrate that even our sense of free will prove to be a powerful illusion (Kuhn 2019). Studying the ease with which a magician can manipulate our conscious experience is providing intriguing and, at times, unsettling new insights into the human mind.

A scientific study of magic shows us that our true perception is far removed from reality than we assume. How can we get back to perceptions of reality, which are more accurate?

Studying the ease with which a magician can manipulate our conscious experience is providing intriguing and, at times, unsettling new insights into the human mind. A scientific study of magic shows us that our true perception is far removed from reality than we assume. How can we get back to perceptions of reality, which are more accurate?

55

Beer to Preserve Society

How does a society preserve its identity and pass on its visions to others? Interestingly, one of ways is through coming together, sharing the stories and planning for the future. A little beer will help in this process!

So, the questions we ask in this section are: What keeps a society together? How does a society evolve naturally? How are intoxicants part of a culture? What can create shared identities and binding loyalties?

About thousands of years ago, the Wari empire stretched across Peru in South America. At its height, it covered an area the size of the Eastern seaboard of the US from New York City to Jacksonville. It lasted for 500 years, from 600 to 1100 AD, before eventually giving rise to the Inca. That is a long time for an empire to remain intact and archaeologists are studying remnants of the Wari culture to see what kept it ticking. A new scientific study found an important factor that might have helped: a steady supply of beer, reports *ScienceDaily* (Field Museum 2019).

"This study helps us understand how beer fed the creation of complex political organizations," says Ryan Williams, an associate curator and Head of Anthropology at the Field Museum and the lead author of the new study in *Sustainability*. "We were able to apply new technologies to capture information about how ancient beer was produced and what it meant to societies in the past "(Field Museum 2019).

Nearly twenty years ago, Williams, Donna Nash (Field Museum and University of North Carolina Greensboro) and their team discovered an ancient Wari brewery in Cerro Baúl in the mountains of Southern Peru. "It was like a microbrewery in some respects. It was a production house, but the brewhouses and taverns would have been right next door," explains Williams. And since the beer they brewed, a light, sour beverage called chicha, was only good for about a week after being made, it wasn't shipped offsite – people had to come to festivals at Cerro Baúl to drink it. These festivals were important to Wari society – between one and two hundred local political elites would attend and they would drink chicha from three-foot-tall ceramic vessels decorated to look like Wari gods and leaders. "People would have come into this site, in these festive moments, in order to recreate and reaffirm their affiliation with these Wari lords and maybe bring tribute and pledge loyalty to the Wari state," says Williams. In short, "beer helped keep the empire together," he concluded (Field Museum 2019).

To learn more about the beer that played such an important role in Wari society, Williams and his co-authors analyzed pieces of ceramic beer vessels from Cerro Baúl. They used several techniques, including one that involved shooting a laser at a shard of a beer vessel to remove a tiny bit of material and then heating that dust to the temperature of the surface of the sun to break down the molecules that make it up. From there, the researchers were able to tell what atomic elements make up the sample and how many – information that told researchers exactly where the clay came from and what the beer was made of.

"The cool thing about this study is that we're getting down to the atomic level. We're counting atoms in the pores of the ceramics or trying to reconstruct and count the masses of molecules that were in the original drink from a thousand years ago that got embedded into the empty spaces between grains of clay in the ceramic vessels and that's what's telling us the new information about what the beer was made of and where the ceramic vessels were produced," says Williams. "It's really new information at the molecular level that is giving archaeologists this new insight into the past."

To check that the ingredients in chicha could indeed be transferred to the brewing vessels, the researchers worked with Peruvian brewers to recreate the brewing process. “Making chicha is a complicated process that requires experience and expertise. The experiments taught us a lot about what making chicha would look like in the ruins of a building and how much labor and time went into the process,” says Donna Nash, an adjunct curator at the Field Museum and professor at the University of North Carolina Greensboro, who led the brewing recreation.

By looking at the chemical makeup of traces of beer left in the vessels and at the chemical makeup of the clay vessels themselves, the team found two important things. One, the vessels were made of clay that came from nearby and two, the beer was made of pepper berries, an ingredient that can grow even during a drought. Both these things would help make for a steady beer supply – even if a drought made it hard to grow other chicha ingredients like corn, or if changes in trade made it hard to get clay from far away, vessels of pepper berry chicha would still be readily available.

The authors of the study argue that this steady supply of beer could have helped keep Wari society stable. The Wari empire was huge and made up of different groups of people from all over Peru. “We think these institutions of brewing and then serving the beer really formed a unity among these populations, it kept people together,” says Williams (Field Museum 2019).

The study’s implications about how shared identity and cultural practices help to stabilize societies are increasingly relevant today. “This research is important because it helps us understand how institutions create the binds that tie together people from very diverse constituencies and very different backgrounds,” says Williams. “Without them, large political entities begin to fragment and break up into much smaller things,” (Field Museum 2019).

Shared identity and cultural practices help to stabilize societies are increasingly relevant today. This research is important because it helps us understand how institutions create the binds that tie together people from remarkably diverse constituencies and very different backgrounds.

56

Kurien Kunnumpuram: Committed to the Country and the Church

In the last article on this section, we look on one creative and committed person, who was involved with both religion and politics. Who was devoted to the Church and the Country, India: Prof Kunnumpuram.

A new theological book, *Committed to the Church and the Country: Exploring the Theological Contributions of Prof. Dr Kurien Kunnumpuram SJ*, explores the commitment of a Christian to his country (Pandikattu and Mathew 2019). Prof Kunnumpuram Professor, Jnana Deepa (JD), Pune, has specialised on Second Vatican Council (1962-65), which has radically revolutionised the Church. He had been teaching various subjects like Theological Anthropology, Ecclesiology and Priesthood for more than thirty years. After his retirement, he has been editing two journals, *Jnana deepa: Pune Journal of Religious Studies* and *Asian Journal of Religious Studies*, through which he has communicated liberating and humanising visions of the Church.

Dr Kunnumpuram is a versatile personality: a committed professor of theology, creative thinker, prolific writer, gentle mentor and compassionate guide to many people. As a professor of theology, he has been the pioneer to introduce and enable the vision of Vatican II to the Indian Church. As a thinker, he has contributed significantly to an Indian theology that is both contextual and relevant. As a writer, he has founded *Jnana deepa: Pune Journal of Religious Studies* and edited *Asian Journal for Religious Studies*, besides his numerous books. As a mentor, he has been inspiring a countless number of students in their academic and affective progress. As a guide, he has been accompanying numerous persons in their intellectual and spiritual journey. In short, he has been a critical, creative and gentle personality who has touched the lives of many people respectfully and reverentially! He cherished freedom, affirmed the dignity and accepted others as they are and rejoiced in the happiness of others!

Coming to the academic part: as a theologian and teacher, he has been pleading for a Church that is more human and promoting human persons who are more liberated and liberating. He has been consistently pleading for a spirituality that is rooted in a personal encounter with God and in the deepest human values! One of his last contributions to theology has been single-handedly editing the collected works of Samuel Rayan, a six-volume work. A remarkable contribution to the Indian Church!

Considering his invaluable contribution to Indian Christian Theology, a compilation of articles has been brought out in his honour. The articles are related to the themes that have been dear to Kurien: Church, the nation, human beings and spirituality. Some articles are based on his chosen writings and are meant to continue the path of theological reflection on the Indian soil.

After elaborate planning and exchange of views, the seminar was organised at Kozhikode (Calicut), Kerala, on October 17-18, 2018, Kurien had a stroke on 17 November 2017 and was bedridden and could not take part in this Seminar which he was eagerly preparing for. Unfortunately, just five days after the seminar, on Sunday, October 23, 2018, Kurien passed away peacefully.Kunnumpuram has been a person passionately devoted to the church and the nation. He was rooted in the rich heritage of India and that of the church. He embraced the values, vision and ethos of India and the church. He felt entirely at home in the

Indian culture and Christian fellowship. His was truly a life of devotion to India and commitment to the church. We hope that the readers of this book will be good citizens and committed Christians!

In his life as well as writings, he draws on hope, joy and freedom, which remain the core values Kurien nourished, both as a Christian and as an author, as elaborated in his last book. It visualises a Christian living that is rooted in Christ joyfully and lovingly and at the same time affirms the freedom, dignity and worth of fellow human beings!

In his life as well as writings, Prof. Kunnumpuram draws on hope, joy and freedom, which remain his core values, both as a Christian and as an author, as elaborated in his last book. It visualises a Christian living that is rooted in Christ joyfully and lovingly and at the same time affirms the freedom, dignity and worth of fellow human beings.

PART - IX
Promoting Social Commitment

57

Demagogues and Mass Movements

After having paid attention to the society, we are interested to change the society for the better. Promoting social values and commitment to people, especially the poor and underprivileged is part of our noble attempt to be sisters and brothers to one another. The first article talks about threatening demagogues and dangerous mass movements.

When we are witnessing the rise of demagogues and radical movements all over the world, it is useful to reflect on their origin and religious basis. The social philosophy Eric Hofer has given us an illuminating analysis of such mass movements and their leaders in his *The True Believer: Thoughts on the Nature of Mass Movements* (Hofer 2002).

In this critically acclaimed work, Hoffer lays bare the thoughts, emotions and justifications that go through the minds of the masses who form such movement. The following excerpts from the *True Believer* selected by social activist and writer Rohit Kumar may be helpful to understand the dangerous phenomenon of mass movements on the rise in recent times in America, Europe and India.

Such leaders are not visionaries. "The quality of ideas seems to play a minor role in mass movement leadership. What counts is the arrogant gesture, the complete disregard of the opinion of others, the singlehanded defiance of the world" (Kumar 2016).

They look for personal glory, often manifested in extreme narcissism: "Glory is largely a theatrical concept. There is no striving for glory without a vivid awareness of an audience... The desire to escape or camouflage their unsatisfactory selves develops in the frustrated a facility for pretending – for making a show – and also a readiness to identify themselves wholly with an imposing spectacle."

Hoffer also refers to the masses who hunger for such a leader: "For men to plunge headlong into an undertaking of vast change, they must be intensely discontented yet not destitute and they must have the feeling that by the possession of some potent doctrine, infallible leader or some new technique they have access to a source of irresistible power. They must also have an extravagant conception of the prospects and potentialities of the future. Finally, they must be wholly ignorant of the difficulties involved in their vast undertaking. Experience is a handicap" (Kumar 2016).

According to him, all mass movements are, to an extent, religious because they promote powerful, sometimes illogical doctrines that require a dose of faith. And they inspire almost blind devotion. "Faith in a holy cause is to a considerable extent a substitute for the lost faith in ourselves." So "the facts on which the true believer bases his conclusions must not be derived from his experience or observation but from holy writ." So, it is no wonder that "mass movements aggressively promote the use of doctrines that elevate faith over reason and serve as fact-proof screens between the faithful and the realities of the world."

Further, Hoffer notes how mass movements tend to glorify the past and deprecate the present, done normally by the best and the worst people in the group. "The game of history is usually played by the best and the worst over the heads of the majority in the middle. The reason that the inferior elements of a nation can exert a marked influence on its course is that they are wholly without reverence toward the present. They see their lives and the present as spoiled beyond remedy and they are ready to waste and wreck both: hence their recklessness and their will to chaos and anarchy" (Kumar 2016).

Hoffer warns of the need and dangers of demonizing some sections of the group. Mass Movements always externalize the enemy: "Hatred is the most accessible and comprehensive of all the unifying agents. Mass movements can rise and spread without belief in a god, but never without a belief in a devil."

Perhaps the best way to deal with such dangerous movements is "to encourage individualism, independent thinking," according to Rohit Kumar. "To wrong those we hate is to add fuel to our hatred. Conversely, to treat an enemy with magnanimity is to blunt our hatred for him" (Kumar 2016). Can we realise the danger the demagogues are doing to our society and at the same time not fall into their trap? We can only counter their techniques by creative thinking, individual initiative, collective vision and peaceful protests.

> "To wrong those we hate is to add fuel to our hatred. Conversely, to treat an enemy with magnanimity is to blunt our hatred for him" Can we realise the danger the demagogues are doing to our society and at the same time not fall into their trap? We can only counter their techniques by creative thinking, individual initiative, collective vision and peaceful protests.

58

Operation Sulaimani: Responding to Physical Hunger

We look at one specific example of social concern, to feed the hungry. We do have the sources to feed all the people in our beloved world. A straightforward illustration follows.

Food is obviously a basic necessity. Recently a noble venture has enabled to give free food to the needy: 'Operation Sulaimani.' Launched by district administration and Kerala Hotel and Restaurants Association, Kozhikode, this venture enables those without resources to have a meal with dignity. It provides free food to the needy, with no questions asked (TNN 2015).

Malayalam movie "Ustad Hotel", where the protagonist, a hotel owner in Kozhikode, keeps a part of his income to feed the hungry, has inspired this move. The project aims to act as an intermediary between those who are willing to give and the less fortunate who must depend on others for a meal.

"Kozhikode is a melting pot. Influence of the Portuguese, Arabs and French is reflected in its food varieties. Sulaimani (black tea laced with cardamom) has an Arab touch and is usually taken by the people of Malabar after a sumptuous lunch or dinner," said Dr M K Muneer, minister for social justice, reports *The Times of India* (TNN 2015).

N Prasanth, District Collector, Kozhikode, said: "If you are hungry, you should get food. To penetrate the (scheme's) reach, we gave free coupons attached to newspapers which people could give to anyone they thought would require them. Everything is volunteer-based and we don't even charge an administrative fee." As per the initial plan, around 1,000 people were to get food per day. "The price of the food will be covered through sponsorship," the collector said (TNN 2015).

"We cannot ask a hungry person to get his hunger attested by a certified gazetted officer! That is why we insisted on the philosophy that 'no questions will be asked'. If you ask for a food coupon, you will get it, it is as dignified as that," added the Collector.

Most restaurant owners say the scheme has given them the opportunity to help many without losing out on revenue. Offers from corporate sponsors have been turned down in favour of crowd funding to give the citizens of Kozhikode a sense of ownership of the scheme. A substantial amount has been collected till now through drop boxes placed at various restaurants. Just two days after the launch of Operation Sulaimani, the Collector got a massive one crore donation offer, which he refused.

The team believes that the spirit of Operation Sulaimani lies in the collective responsibility taken by the people to care for each other rather than an act of benevolence by any individual or organization. This collective spirit has proved to be indeed powerful by feeding 9000 people in the last one year, not running out of funds and not showing signs that the city's good spirit will allow them to run out too.

One of the striking aspects of Operation Sulaimani is the fact that it gets fulfilled within the capabilities of existing systems. No big kitchens to feed the hungry were built and no massive funds were sought in the name of hunger eradication. By leading people to any restaurant in any part of the city, it blended the cause into the everyday function of Kozhikode's restaurants.

The District Collector adds, "There is no food wastage, nor do we have to worry about the safety of the food. If we had chosen to build a large kitchen to supply free food, we would have all these problems. But we just decided to use the existing system and make the best use of it" (TNN 2015).

One of the restaurants in the vicinity of the city mental hospital feeds several people who come in with coupons. The restaurant owner says his life has never felt so blessed.

This truly noble venture needs multiplication. At the same time, we also need genuine centres where healthy spiritual food is served – freely and joyfully! Physical hunger must be freely satisfied. So is also spiritual thirst!

Sulaimani is truly noble venture and needs multiplication. At the same time, we also need genuine centres where healthy spiritual food is served – freely and joyfully! Physical hunger must be freely satisfied. So is also spiritual thirst!

59

Superstitions as a Global Phenomenon

Another problematic case is the rise of superstition, both in thought and action. They challenge the way we treat each other and respect each other. So we look at how highly educated people also can believe in act according to superstitions.

Is religion related to superstition? Are there other areas where superstitious or illogical beliefs dominate? According to a recent UNI India report, "superstition a global phenomenon, not restrained by barriers like intellect, religion, boundaries." The report says that even highly qualified people, including those with University-level science education, often talk absurd things, have faith in superstition and irrational ideas and fail to listen to the voice of reason and logic.

Psychologists are trying to understand the cognitive processes, ideologies, cultural moorings and conspiracy beliefs that cause smart people to resist scientific messages. Using surveys, experiments, observational studies and meta-analyses, the researchers capture an emerging theoretical frontier in order to make "science communication efforts smarter and more effective" (Society for Personality and Social Psychology 2017).

One paradoxical or striking feature of people who are against science is that they are often just as educated and just as interested in science, just as others who support science. So the real problem "is not about whether they are exposed to information, but about whether the information is processed in a balanced way."

Researcher Matthew Hornsey from University of Queensland describes this phenomenon as "thinking like a lawyer." Here people cherry-pick which pieces of information to pay attention to "in order to reach conclusions that they want to be true". "We find that people will take a flight from facts to protect all kinds of belief including their religious belief, their political beliefs and even simple personal beliefs such as whether they are good at choosing a web browser," says Troy Campbell of University of Oregon (Society for Personality and Social Psychology 2017).

Dan Kahan of Yale University agrees with these findings, holding that "the deposition is to construe evidence in identity-congruent rather than truth-congruent ways, a state of disorientation that is pretty symmetric across the political spectrum. It may be noted that merely talking about "evidence" or "data" does not typically change a sceptic's mind about a topic, whether it is climate change, genetically modified organisms, or vaccines. The researchers found that in real life people "use science and fact to support their particular opinion and will downplay what they don't agree with."

"Where there is conflict over societal risks - from climate change to nuclear-power safety to impacts of gun control laws, both sides invoke the mantel of science," says Kahan. "We find that people treat facts as relevant more when the facts tend to support their opinions," says Campbell. When the facts are against their opinions, they do not necessarily deny them, but they relativise or trivialise them.

"One approach to deal with science scepticism is to identify the underlying motivations or "attitude roots," as Hornsey describes in his recent research. "Rather than taking on people's surface attitudes directly, tailor the message so that it aligns with their motivation," he suggests.

Kahan's recent research shows that a person's level of scientific curiosity could help promote more open-minded engagement. They also found that people, who enjoyed surprising findings, even if it was counter to their political beliefs, were more open to the new information (Society for Personality and Social Psychology 2017).

The above research acknowledges that superstition is not only limited to religion, but it can spread itself to politics, economics and even science. We need to check our fundamental assumption that we are open to facts and will readily replace beliefs based on facts. Even in science it does not happen.

Knowing this we can learn to be extra cautious in seeing how far facts or evidence shape our everyday lives. Realising that there are many non-rational elements that shape our belief or vision, we need to be extra cautious to deal with truth at the personal level and even more at the societal level. Only then can we foster a society free from different dimensions of superstitions.

> Knowing that superstitious beliefs are present in science and religion, we can learn to be extra cautious in seeing how far facts or evidence shape our everyday lives. Realising that there are many non-rational elements that shape our belief or vision, we need to be extra cautious to deal with truth at the personal level and even more at the societal level. Only then can we foster a society free from different dimensions of superstitions.

60

The Missing Child

While dealing with social concern, one important factor is the child, "the father of man" (Wordsworth). The concern for them is truly relevant for our India.

Why don't we care for our own children? asks Sonia Faleiro (2012), author of *Beautiful Thing: Inside the Secret World of Bombay's Dance Bars*, writing in *The New York Times* (Faleiro 201).

She reports an incident of April 2017, when 13-year-old Savitri was walking with her mother in Uttar Pradesh. She was carrying a flask of tea to her father, a labourer at a brick kiln, when five men abducted her into a moving jeep. One of them was from their village.

When Savitri's father heard of it, he hitchhiked to the police station, since he couldn't afford to take the bus. The officers set out to look for the man who had been recognized. Since they could not find him, they demolished his hut. That was the end of the matter!

One of the officers admitted that he did not think they could have done anything more. "Girls run away," he told Faleiro, with a shrug. Savitri became another statistic – actually, she *did not even* become a statistic. Missing from home and then absent on paper, the teenager is a phantom. And she is just one among very many, notes Faleiro (2017).

It is difficult to get reliable figures about how many Indian children go missing, but the scale of the problem appears greater. According to the country's Ministry of Women and Child Development, 242,938 children disappeared between 2012 and 2017. But according to TrackChild, a government database, nearly 237,040 went missing between 2012 and 2014 alone.

Activists claim that "under-registration – as well as underreporting – of missing children is a chronic problem, estimate that the real numbers are much higher." According to Bhuwan Ribhu, a lawyer with *Bachpan Bachao Andolan*, an anti-trafficking organization, the figure may reach 500,000 a year, an incredibly high number.

Several factors account for the disappearances, but perhaps "none more so than destitution." At least half of India's minors are said to live in acute poverty. Looking for a missing child requires time, manpower and resources and the police force in India is short on all of those. So many missing children's cases are not even reported to the police.

Abhijit Banerjee, Director, Abdul Latif Jameel Poverty Action Lab, admitted that "parents may be reluctant to report children who ran away as a result of abuse, sexual and otherwise – which I think is rampant." Some parents sell their children or, deliberately allow unwanted daughters to stray in busy marketplaces. Really tragic!

Some poor children voluntarily approach people they think are labour contractors, offering their services in exchange for an advance and fall prey to trafficking networks.

The 2017 Trafficking in Persons Report, of US State Department, says that, "Experts estimate millions of women and children are victims of sex trafficking in India." According to the 2016 Global Slavery Index, "India had the largest number of slaves of any country in the world." Again, "the lack of hard data about the issue is an issue in itself," notes Faleiro (2017).

High Court in New Delhi, where the problem of missing children is especially acute, declared in 2016 the subject to be of "extreme importance," calling it "as bad as terrorism." The court upbraided the local police for not recovering the lost children. Of the 26,761 children who have gone missing in the city during the last five years, only 37 percent have been traced so far.

According to TrackChild, a government database with searchable photos of children who were formally reported as missing, between 2012 and 2014, the police filed First Information Reports in only 40 per cent of cases. "Why are they so lifeless, so disinterested?" the Delhi court asked. To many Indians, according to Rishi Kant of Shakti Vahini, it is as if these children "are not our own." We must acknowledge that "child is the father of men," with William Wordsworth. A society that ignores its children ignores itself perilously.

To many Indians it is as if these children "are not our own." We must acknowledge that "child is the father of men," with William Wordsworth. A society that ignores its children ignores itself perilously.

61

The Poetry of the Vulnerable

Raising our voice for the poor and underprivilege is also part of our social concern and commitment. Poetry can help us in this venture. So, in this part we see how two young ladies speak for their vulnerable communities.

The questions we ask are: How do poets express the violence and vulnerabilities of their communities? Where lies the power of poetry? Two young poets show us the way.

The young Kashmiri poet, Nighat Sahiba became a close friend of Jacinta Kerketta, an Adivasi poet from West Singhbhum district, Jharkhand. A conversation with the two friends, who belong to states and communities torn by violence, turns into a fascinating discussion on the power of words and the role of poetry, writes Kavitha Muralidharan in *The Huffington Post* (Muralidharan 2019).

Jacinta, who hails from the Kurukhar community (also called Oraon), speaks the Kurukh language. "The name Oraon was given to us by the Hindu mainstream society to degrade us. I would like to identify myself as belonging to Kurukhar community," said Jacinta.

She writes in Hindi. "People are never worried about why my mother tongue is disappearing but when I say I write in Hindi, they have questions. I write in Hindi because I want to speak to the perpetrators of injustice and violence on my community in their own language. I write in their language so they will know what we think of them," she said.

Jacinta's poems are brutally honest about the struggles Adivasi communities face in the face of the onslaught of 'development'. Her poetry is a powerful account of the injustices perpetrated on the community. For example: My Pet Dog was murdered/ For the sole reason/ That it had barked on seeing a danger. / It was declared rabid/ Before being killed.

Nighat is clear: "A language is more than a mode of communication. It has a culture to it, a history. When I write in Kashmiri or Urdu, I make a very emphatic statement. Like Jacinta says, there is no word for rape in Kashmiri. We had such rich culture and yet look at what we are forced to suffer today," she said (Muralidharan 2019).

When Jacinta first came in conflict with power and saw how her community was persecuted for no fault of theirs, she decided to write. "My uncle was murdered by dominant caste members when I was in school and the mainstream media reported it as human sacrifice made by our community. That is when I decided I should be a journalist. But later, I realised I am not doing much as a journalist. But poetry has given me a voice that is heard. I have travelled many countries, picked many awards and continue fighting for my community. Poetry changed my life," she added (Muralidharan 2019).

Both Jacinta and Nighat are torchbearers in the environment that they live in. "I feel responsible in that I am an icon of sorts in my community. ... They have seen that my poetry has taken me to places. Now they know what it means to express ourselves in the mainstream. Our voices are beginning to be counted and it is a huge change," said Jacinta.

Nighat is among the few women poets in Kashmir: "It is possible that the voices got lost, that the poetry had got vanished. In a place of conflict, women are first affected. They are most vulnerable, yet the vulnerabilities are never allowed to express themselves in powerful ways" (Muralidharan 2019).

Both Jacinta and Nighat believe in the "poet's obligation to be a witness to the times they live in," writes Muralidharan. To Jacinta, it is not just about being a witness but being part of the change. "We take our verses from common people, yet how many writers stand with common people when it comes to issues? How many writers want to go out there and be part of their struggles? I want to be known as people's poet. That is where I come from, that is where I belong to." Poets have something prophetic to contribute to society.

"We take our verses from common people, yet how many writers stand with common people when it comes to issues? How many writers want to go out there and be part of their struggles? I want to be known as people's poet. That is where I come from, that is where I belong to."

62

Political Identity: Coming Apart

All around the way, we see frightening prospects of tension between politicians and the people. In this case we take the specific case of not Europe, the mother of democratic experiments and liberal ideas.

Europe 'coming apart before our eyes', claims 30 top intellectuals. Liberal values in Europe face a challenge "not seen since the 1930s", leading intellectuals from 21 countries have opined, as the UK moves towards Brexit and nationalists look set to make sweeping gains in EU parliamentary elections.

The 30 writers, consisting historians and Nobel laureates declared in a manifesto that Europe as an idea was "coming apart before our eyes". They add: "We must now will Europe or perish beneath the waves of populism." They go on: "We must rediscover political voluntarism or accept that resentment, hatred and their cortege of sad passions will surround and submerge us."

Bernard-Henri Lévy, Milan Kundera, Salman Rushdie, Elfriede Jelinek, Orhan Pamuk and 25 others write of their regret that Europe has been "abandoned from across the Channel" – an apparent reference to the drawn-out Brexit process that has arguably brought Anglo-European relations to their lowest point since the second world war, write Jon Henley and Mark Rice-Oxley in *The Guardian* (Rice-Oxley 2019).

And they say that unless efforts are made to combat a rising tide of populism, the EU elections will be "the most calamitous that we have ever known: victory for the wreckers; disgrace for those who still believe in the legacy of Erasmus, Dante, Goethe and Comenius; disdain for intelligence and culture; explosions of xenophobia and antisemitism; disaster".

They are afraid that "Europe as an idea, as will and representation, is coming apart before our eyes," the text reads.

The 800-word letter was drafted by the French philosopher Bernard-Henri Lévy. Salman Rushdie, one of the signatories, asserted: "Europe is in greater danger now than at any time in the last 70 years and if one believes in that idea it's time to stand up and be counted.

"In the UK, I hope parliament may yet have the courage to call for a second referendum. That could rescue the country from the calamity of Brexit and go a long way towards rescuing the EU as well."

Orhan Pamuk, a Turkish novelist, 2006 Nobel Laureate in Literature, said the idea of Europe was also important to non-western countries. "Without the idea of Europe, freedom, women's rights, democracy, egalitarianism is hard to defend in my part of the world."

They add: "The historical success of Europe made it easier to defend these ideas and values which are crucial to humanity all over the world," he said. "There is no Europe besides these values except the Europe of tourism and business. Europe is not geography first but these ideas. This idea of Europe is under attack" (Rice-Oxley 2019).

Euroscepticism and nationalism are on the rise. Matteo Salvini of Italy's far-right League has described the vote as a straight choice between "the Europe of the elites, banks, finance, immigration and precarious work" and that of "the people and of labour". Hungary's prime minister, Viktor Orbán, has said the elections are a chance to bid farewell "to liberal democracy".

The 30 intellectuals did not make any practical calls to action, the manifesto's signatories said they "refuse to resign themselves to this looming catastrophe," but are ready to fight for "a new battle for civilisation," reports *The Guardian.*

Despite its "mistakes, lapses and occasional acts of cowardice", Europe remains "the second home of every free man and woman on the planet", they say, noting with regret the widely held but mistaken belief of their generation that "the continent would come together on its own, without our labour" (Rice-Oxley 2019).

Pro-Europeans "no longer have a choice", they say. "We must sound the alarm against the arsonists of soul and spirit that, from Paris to Rome, with stops in Barcelona, Budapest, Dresden, Vienna, or Warsaw, are playing with the fire of our freedoms.

Can we say the same thing about our own motherland? About the world at large? We need to protect democracy, free speech and egalitarianism.

> "Without the idea of Europe, freedom, women's rights, democracy, egalitarianism is hard to defend in my part of the world."

63

Grief as Deep Activism

Confronted with the sad and painful situation of our own sisters, we feel helpless. Grieved. We see how grief could be the basis for a genuine commitment to others and beginning of true activism.

The American poet Priscilla Denise Levertov has a brief, but an illuminating poem about grief. *"To speak of sorrow/ works upon it/ moves it from its/ crouched place barring/ the way to and from the soul's hall."*

It is our unexpressed sorrows, the congested stories of loss, when left unattended, that block our access to the soul. To be able to freely move in and out of the soul's inner chambers, we must first clear the way. This requires finding meaningful ways to speak of sorrow, writes Francis Weller in *Ritesofpassage* (Weller 2019).

The territory of grief is heavy. Even the word carries weight. Grief comes from the Latin, *gravis*, meaning, heavy, from which we get gravity. We use the term *gravitas* to speak of a quality in some people who carry the weight of the world with a dignified bearing. And so it is, when we learn to accompany our grief with dignity.

Freeman House (2000), in his elegant book, *Totem Salmon,* shared, "In one ancient language, the word memory derives from a word meaning mindful, in another from a word to describe a witness, in yet another it means, at root, to grieve. To witness mindfully is to grieve for what has been lost" (Weller 2019). That is the intent and soul purpose of grief.

No one escapes suffering in this life. None of us is exempt from loss, pain, illness and death. Yet, how is it that we have so little understanding of these essential experiences? How is it we have attempted to keep grief separated from our lives and only begrudgingly acknowledge its presence in the most obvious of times? "If sequestered pain made a sound," Stephen Levine suggests, "the atmosphere would be humming all the time."

It feels somewhat daunting to step off into the depths of grief and suffering, yet I do not know of any more appropriate way to continue our journey of reclaiming the indigenous soul than by spending time at the grief shrine. Without some measure of intimacy with grief, our capacity to be with any other emotion or experience in our life is greatly compromised.

Coming to trust this descent into the dark waters is not easy. Yet without this passageway being successfully transited, we lack the tempering that comes only from such a dropping. What do we find there? Darkness, moistness that turns our eyes wet and our faces into streams. We find the bodies of forgotten ancestors, ancient remnants of trees and animals, those that have come before and lead us back to where we have come from. This descent is a passage into what we are, creatures of the earth.

Grief is a an immensely powerful form of deep activism. If we refuse or neglect the responsibility for drinking the tears of the world, her losses and deaths cease to be registered by the ones meant to be the receptors of that information (Weller 2019). It is our job to feel these losses and to mourn them. It is our job to openly grieve for the loss of wetlands, the destruction of forest systems, the decay of whale populations, the erosion of soft and on and on.

It is sad that we know the litany of loss, but we have collectively neglected our response to this emptying of our world. We need to see and participate in grief rituals in every part of this country. Imagine the power of our voices and tears being heard across the continent. I believe the wolves and coyotes would howl with us, the cranes, egrets and owls would screech, the willows would bend closer to the ground and together the great transforming could happen to us and our great grief cry could happen to the worlds beyond.

Poets and prophets have come to realize the profound wisdom in grief. May we too, come to know this place of grace inside this dark evergreen.

> Grief is an immensely powerful form of deep activism. If we refuse or neglect the responsibility for drinking the tears of the world, her losses and deaths cease to be registered by the ones meant to be the receptors of that information.

64

The Harmful Effects of Mindfulness

In taking up social issues and standing for the rights of fellow human beings, we have to face a painful and desperate situation. In such cases stressing too much on mindfulness and inward prayer may be counter-productive and harmful.

Mindfulness has gone mainstream, with a celebrity endorsement from Oprah Winfrey and Goldie Hawn. Meditation coaches, monks and neuroscientists went to Davos to impart the finer points to CEOs attending the World Economic Forum. The founders of the mindfulness movement have grown evangelical. Prophesying that its hybrid of science and meditative discipline "has the potential to ignite a universal or global renaissance", the inventor of Mindfulness-Based Stress Reduction (MBSR), Jon Kabat-Zinn, has bigger ambitions than conquering stress. Mindfulness, he proclaims, "may actually be the only promise the species and the planet have for making it through the next couple of hundred years".

The conspiracy of mindfulness: So, what exactly is this magic panacea? In 2014, *Time magazine* put a youthful blonde woman on its cover, with the words: "The Mindful Revolution." The accompanying feature described a signature scene from the standardised course teaching MBSR: eating a raisin very slowly. "The ability to focus for a few minutes on a single raisin isn't silly if the skills it requires are the keys to surviving and succeeding in the 21st century," the author explained (Purser 2019).

But anything that offers success in our unjust society without trying to change it is not revolutionary – it just helps people cope. In fact, it could also be making things worse. Instead of encouraging radical action, mindfulness says the causes of suffering are disproportionately inside us, not in the political and economic frameworks that shape how we live. And yet mindfulness zealots believe that paying closer attention to the present moment without passing judgment has the revolutionary power to transform the whole world. It's magical thinking on steroids, writes Ronald Purser in *The Guardian* (Purser 2019).

The fundamental message of the mindfulness movement is that the underlying cause of dissatisfaction and distress is in our heads. By failing to pay attention to what actually happens in each moment, we get lost in regrets about the past and fears for the future, which make us unhappy. Kabat-Zinn, who is often labelled the father of modern mindfulness, calls this a "thinking disease". Learning to focus turns down the volume on circular thought, so Kabat-Zinn's diagnosis is that our "entire society is suffering from attention deficit disorder – big time". Other sources of cultural malaise are not discussed here.

Mindfulness advocates, perhaps unwittingly, are providing support for the status quo. Rather than discussing how attention is monetised and manipulated by corporations such as Google, Facebook, Twitter and Apple, they locate the crisis in our minds. It is not the nature of the capitalist system that is inherently problematic; rather, it is the failure of individuals to be mindful and resilient in a precarious and uncertain economy. Then they sell us solutions that make us contented, mindful capitalists!

Mindfulness, like positive psychology and the broader happiness industry, has depoliticised stress. If we are unhappy about being unemployed, losing our health insurance and seeing our children incur massive debt through college loans, it is our responsibility to learn to be more mindful. Kabat-Zinn assures us that "happiness is an inside job" that simply requires us to attend to the present moment mindfully and purposely without judgment.

Another vocal promoter of meditative practice, the neuroscientist Richard Davidson, contends that "wellbeing is a skill" that can be trained, like working out one's biceps at the gym. The so-called mindfulness revolution meekly accepts the dictates of the marketplace. Guided by a therapeutic ethos aimed at enhancing the mental and emotional resilience of individuals, it endorses neoliberal assumptions that everyone is free to choose their responses, manage negative emotions and "flourish" through various modes of self-care. Framing what they offer in this way, most teachers of mindfulness rule out a curriculum that critically engages with causes of suffering in the structures of power and economic systems of capitalist society, holds Purser (2019).

The Slovenian philosopher Slavoj Žižek has analysed this trend very critically. As he sees it, mindfulness is "establishing itself as the hegemonic ideology of global capitalism", by helping people "to fully participate in the capitalist dynamic while retaining the appearance of mental sanity".

By deflecting attention from the social structures and material conditions in a capitalist culture, mindfulness is easily co-opted. Google's former in-house mindfulness tsar Chade-Meng Tan admonished. "Search inside yourself," he counselled colleagues and readers – for there, not in corporate culture – lies the source of your problems, points out Purser (2019).

The rhetoric of "self-mastery", "resilience" and "happiness" assumes wellbeing is simply a matter of developing a skill. Personal troubles are never attributed to political or socioeconomic conditions but are always psychological in nature and diagnosed as pathologies (Purser 2019). Society, therefore, needs therapy, not radical change. This is perhaps why mindfulness initiatives have become so attractive to government policymakers. Societal problems rooted in inequality, racism, poverty, addiction and deteriorating mental health can be reframed in terms of individual psychology, requiring therapeutic help.

> Mindfulness is "establishing itself as the hegemonic ideology of global capitalism", by helping people "to fully participate in the capitalist dynamic while retaining the appearance of mental sanity".

65

Shakespeare: Telling the Universal Truths about Humanity

Poetry and politics go together. Writers and activists have many things in common. Shakespeare, one of the most insightful English writers, shows how his writings bring out the universal paradoxical trues about us!

William Shakespeare (1564?-1616), inimitable in so many ways, is said to have died on his birthday, 23 April, 400 years ago. So this is an occasion to celebrate this renowned English playwright's 450th birthday and 400th death anniversary. Shakespeare is a writer whose body of works is considered the greatest in the history of English literature, still speaks to us unerringly with universal truths about the human condition.

"And since you know you cannot see yourself, so well as by reflection, I, your glass, will modestly discover to yourself, that of yourself which you yet know not of." William Shakespeare's "glass", what he called his "mind's eye", was his mirror on the world. It allowed him, through the artifice of extraordinary intuition and stagecraft, to know us better than we know ourselves.

He still speaks to humans unerringly with universal truths about all our contradictions and complexities, human frailty, weakness and venality. About high politics and "vaulting ambition that overleaps itself" and the most trivial and often most profound aspects of personal relationships.

Above all, he had an exploration of psychology and the unconscious that was years ahead of his time. "The fault, dear Brutus, is not in our stars/ But in ourselves" ("The bard's anniversary," 2016).

None did it, has done it, better. "The play's the thing". It is not just that the play reveals truths, but Shakespeare understood that life itself is a play. "The play 's the thing wherein I'll catch the conscience of the king". "When we are born we cry that we are come to this great stage of fools," and, sure, "life's but a walking shadow, a poor player,/ That struts and frets his hour upon the stage,/ And then is heard."

That ambiguity about reality and illusion is life is central to this playwright's insight. "Are you sure/ That we are awake? It seems to me/ That, yet we sleep, we dream."

And all wrapped up in a prose that is simply sublime, often heart-wrenching, that has given so many words and expressions to the English language that a short paean like this can never do him justice. "Brevity is the soul of wit". And "Though this be madness, yet there is method in 't".

He waxes eloquently on love. "This is the very ecstasy of love". Again, "Doubt that the sun doth move, doubt truth to be a liar, but never doubt I love". We can savour Juliet's experience of total love: "Give me my Romeo. And when I shall die,/ Take him and cut him out in little stars,/ And he will make the face of heaven so fine/ That all the world will be in love with night/ And pay no worship to the garish sun".

He can be very reflective: "To be, or not to be that is the question". "This above all: to thine own self be true". "And it must follow, as the night the day, thou canst not then be false to any man." Again he adds: "There is nothing either good or bad but thinking makes it so" ("The Bard's anniversary," 2016).

He is deeply aware of the human shadows. "The common curse of mankind, - folly and ignorance". "Do you think I am easier to be played on than a pipe?" "I will speak daggers to her but use none". Further, "When sorrows come, they come not single spies, but in battalions".

About human beings he is deeply insightful: “What a piece of work is man! how noble in reason! how infinite in faculty! in form and moving how express and admirable! in action how like an angel! in apprehension how like a god! the beauty of the world, the paragon of animals!” Finally, “While you live tell truth and shame the devil”.

“The play ‘s the thing wherein I’ll catch the conscience of the king”. “When we are born we cry that we are come to this great stage of fools.” “Life’s but a walking shadow, a poor player,/ That struts and frets his hour upon the stage,/ And then is heard.”

PART - X

Discovering the meaning of me in the cosmos

66

Meaning of Being Human

After talking of our commitment to society with devotion and generosity, we return to our own lives that are both meaningful and liberating. In this section we base ourselves on the famous quote: "He who has found a WHY can cope with any HOW."

So, we pose the following questions. What is it that makes us human? Is it language, imagination, morality, or is it that we cook and wear shoes? Or perhaps we are less human than we think since Neanderthal and Denisovan genes can be found in all of us! What is totally unique to human beings? How closely related are we to other species?

There are some fascinating and unexpected answers in the book *How to be Human: Consciousness, Language and 48 More Things that Make You* (Lawton, Graham and Jeremy Webb 2010). The book takes us on a tour around the human body and brain, taking in everything from evolution to email, from the Stone Age to Spotify.

The authors of the book, New Scientist deputy editor Graham Lawton and his colleague Jeremy Webb, ask: How do languages change the way our brains are wired? What can evolutionary theory tell us about who we are attracted to? How does your voice give away clues about your political views, your sexual allure and even your salary? Why is gossip the human version of a gorilla picking fleas from its mate? And how can you live to 100? (Mulligan 2017).

From the body to language, through emotions and possessions, to the most tricky questions about life and death, witty essays in the book fits well with enlightening illustrations that range from how your brain creates the illusion of 'self' to the allure of body odour.

Lawton says the book began with the idea of an alien biologist looking down on the earth – a planet teeming with life, but where one species stands out from the crowd – human beings, says broadcaster Jesse Mulligan in Radio New Zealand (Mulligan 2017).

"The list of things that we can do that no animal has ever achieved ... language, cities, technology, religion, music, art. The list goes on and on and on."

But some of our most sophisticated creations - such as language - are also problematic. Although language seems like it was originally designed to help us communicate, most of the time it divides us as a species, Lawton holds.

Some scientists even suggest this division is intentional." We're a very tribal species. We take almost every opportunity to divide ourselves into smaller and smaller and smaller groups" (Mulligan 2017).

While we are not the only earthlings who laugh – rats laugh when tickled – we're probably the only species to laugh out of politeness, he says. One of Lawton's favourite experiments involves a group of scientists who went out to record 'laughter in the wild', i.e. laughter of human beings in public.

Whenever they heard someone laugh, they went up and asked the person why they were doing it. Many people didn't realise they were laughing and couldn't say why they were laughing; he says.

The conclusion – most 'laughter in the wild' has nothing to do with humour. He adds: "The most banal comments would elicit laughter ... Someone went up to someone else in a shopping mall and said 'When you've finished with your shopping trolley can I use it?' and the person, in response, laughed. That's just not funny … Laughter is a social signal we send to each to say that we're okay" (Mulligan 2017).

Our life of laughter and love is truly nuanced and subtle. We need to acknowledge that there is so much of beauty and depth in ourselves. We are part of an ongoing adventure, which is remarkably complex. There are lots of areas where we can learn from and be impressed. Truly, we can look at ourselves and be in awe and wonder.

This realization should help us to respect ourselves and to treat fellow human beings with dignity. This should enable us to revere nature, that sustains us. Joyfully we can laugh at ourselves and others.

> We are part of an ongoing adventure, which is remarkably complex. Truly, we can look at ourselves and be in awe and wonder. This realization should help us to respect ourselves and to treat fellow human beings with dignity. This should enable us to revere the nature, that sustains us. Joyfully we can laugh at ourselves and others.

67

Being True to Myself

After reflecting on a meaningful life, we seek truthfulness and integrity in our own lives. "To be nobody-but-yourself – in a world which is doing its best, night and day, to make you everybody else – means to fight the hardest battle which any human being can fight," writes Mario Popova of *BrainPickings* (Popova 2017).

No one can build you the bridge on which you and only you, must cross the river of life," wrote the famous German philosopher Friedrich Nietzsche. "The true and durable path into and through experience," Nobel-winning poet Seamus Heaney counselled the young that life "involves being true … to your own solitude, true to your own secret knowledge."

According to Popova, every generation believes that it must battle unprecedented pressures of conformity; that it must fight harder than any previous generation to protect that secret knowledge from which our integrity of selfhood springs. Some of this belief stems from the habitual conceit of a culture blinded by its own bias, "ignorant of the past's contextual analogues." But much of it in the century and a half since Nietzsche and especially in the years since Heaney, is an accurate reflection of the conditions we have created and continually reinforce in our present informational ecosystem – a Pavlovian system of constant feedback, in which the easiest and commonest opinions are most readily rewarded and dissenting voices are most readily punished by the unthinking mob (Popova 2017).

Few people in the two centuries since Emerson issued his exhortation to "trust thyself" have "countered this culturally condoned blunting of individuality" more courageously and consistently than E.E. Cummings (1894–1962) – an artist who never cowered from being his unconventional self because, in the words of his most incisive and competent biographer, he "despised fear and his life was lived in defiance of all who ruled by it."

After his fifty-ninth birthday, a small Michigan newspaper published a short and insightful piece by Cummings under the title "A Poet's Advice to Students," which he himself described as "a cluster of epigrams, forty-nine essays on various subjects, a poem dispraising dogmata and several selections from unfinished plays."

Addressing those who aspire to be poets he writes: "A poet is somebody who feels and who expresses his feelings through words. This may sound easy. It isn't." This is because poetry is genuine feeling. "A lot of people think or believe or know they feel – but that's thinking or believing or knowing; not feeling. And poetry is feeling – not knowing or believing or thinking."

He adds: "Almost anybody can learn to think or believe or know, but not a single human being can be taught to feel. Why? Because whenever you think or you believe or you know, you're a lot of other people: but the moment you feel, you're nobody-but-yourself" (Popova 2017).

So the hardest battle of a poet is to be oneself: "To be nobody-but-yourself – in a world which is doing its best, night and day, to make you everybody else – means to fight the hardest battle which any human being can fight; and never stop fighting."

"It takes courage to grow up and become who you really are," claims Cummings. Poets are called to be true. "As for expressing nobody-but-yourself in words, that means working just a little harder than anybody who isn't a poet can possibly imagine. Why? Because nothing is quite as easy as using words like somebody else. We all of us do exactly this nearly all of the time – and whenever we do it, we're not poets."

And so his advice to all young people who wish to become poets is: "do something easy, like learning how to blow up the world – unless you're not only willing, but glad, to feel and work and fight till you die." Being true to oneself is the hardest thing to do!

> "A poet is somebody who feels and who expresses his feelings through words. This may sound easy. It isn't." This is because poetry is genuine feeling. "A lot of people think or believe or know they feel – but that's thinking or believing or knowing; not feeling. And poetry is feeling – not knowing or believing or thinking."

68

Being Involved with Oneself

After dwelling on meaning and truthfulness, in the last two essays, it is useful to spend some time on our own selves. Do we get involved with our selves, dreams and wishes? Not in a narcissistic or selfish sense, but with an eagerness to know ourselves and to be a friend to ourselves.

How do we recognise the danger and appreciate the opportunities offered by modern technology? Addressing young women graduating from a prestigious school in the Washington, current American Chief Justice, John Roberts, warned that artificial intelligence and big data can alter the way people perceive the world (Wolf 2018).

He noted machines advise lawmakers "what their constituents think, how strongly they feel about particular issues, how best to appeal to them and so on." "Any politician would find it very difficult not to shape his or her message to what constituents want to hear," Roberts said. "Artificial intelligence can change leaders into followers."

Along the same lines, the chief justice warned, private companies can "tell you what to read, watch and listen to, based on what you've read, watched and listened to," as well as match customers to their preferred people and ideas, reports *USA Today* (Wolf 2018).

"The result," he said, "can be a narrowing and over-simplification that is contrary to individuality and creativity." "I worry that we will start thinking like machines," Roberts emphasised.

To combat that trend, he urged the graduate students to take time for solitude, pensive thought and "to stay involved with yourself." "My advice is, when you get to college, to set a little time aside each day to think about things instead of simply acquiring more information. Do not read more, do not research more, do not take notes. Put aside books, papers, computers, telephones. Sit, perhaps just for a half-hour and think about what you're learning."

"If you weren't privileged when you came here, you're privileged now because you have been here," Roberts told the boarding school graduates. "My advice is: Don't act like it."

After the Head of School introduced the 17th chief justice, he noted that he was given only 10 minutes. "I said, 'Ten minutes? How can I communicate all the wisdom that I have acquired over the years in ten minutes?'" Roberts added: "She said, 'Speak very slowly'" (Wolf 2018).

Roberts urged the members of so-called "Generation Z" to be genuinely happy. To drive home this point, he quoted the American Declaration of Independence's promise of "life, liberty and the pursuit of happiness." He added: "You have a patriotic duty to be happy."

And he urged them not to spend all their time communicating with peers, most often on social media. Noting Generation Z also is known for "FOMO – Fear of Missing Out" He affirmed: "You need more time to be alone." Then his final heart-to-heart warning to the students: "What is very interesting can become very creepy, very fast" (Wolf 2018).

The challenge we are faced with is to be deeply involved with oneself, without withdrawing into oneself. In our context of social media and artificial intelligence, it is extremely easy to follow the crowd and to be obsessed with FOMO. This makes all of us passive followers of the system or the machine? The urge to be relevant, contemporary and fashionable can backfire on us since the fashionable never gives us a hold or a grip. It sweeps everything from under our feet!

Can we truly get in touch with ourselves, become involved with our own fears, hopes and joys, so that we can be truly creative and inspiring persons who can profoundly change ourselves and the world? Can we recognize the opportunities and dangers offered by modern technology and lifestyle?

For this we need time spent alone creatively. We need to reflect explore and experience ourselves in our intimate, darkest and brightest moments. Then we can reach out to the others, critically challenging and creatively offering solutions for joy, fulfilment and hope. This demands we need to "speak slowly," and live consciously. We need to be silently involved with ourselves first!

We need time spent alone creatively. We need to reflect explore and experience ourselves in our intimate, darkest and brightest moments. Then we can reach out to the others, critically challenging and creatively offering solutions for joy, fulfilment and hope. This demands we need to "speak slowly," and live consciously. We need to be silently involved with ourselves first!

69

Religion Gives Meaning

In our search for meaning and truth, religions do come to our aid. In fact, religion is the ultimate source of our meaning. So we ask: How does religion give meaning not only to individuals but also to communities? How do shared religious stories build common identities? Neil MacGregor, former director of the National Gallery, London, of the British Museum provides us some valuable insights in his interview to *Mint* (Kohli 2018).

He considers historical objects as "much larger than symbols of national significance and form our collective world heritage. Author of *Living with the Gods* (MacGregor 2019), his approach to religion and culture draws on these historical artefacts and examines their multiple dimensions and the stories they tell of different communities.

He is convinced that religions emerge out of a need to tell stories in order to give meaning to our lives. So, he quotes the well-known novelist and literary critic, Joan Didion, "We tell ourselves stories in order to live". For most of history, the value of the story was the extent to which it enabled us to understand our place in the big scheme of the world. "The difference between a story that was imagined and a story that was historical was not a central one; it was the effect of the story enabling us to live with each other" (Kohli 2018).

The conviction there was only one kind of historical, scientific and verifiable truth was an 18th-century invention. Based on the Enlightenment the Europeans imagined that the church and state were there to oppress the people. From there emerged the further idea if a story was not historically true, then it could have no value.

And this misses a central point that this story does not just have to be the opiate of the masses administered by the powerful, it can also be the strength of the masses. So, according to MacGregor, religion provides us with stories that work to give oppressed people the dignity due to them.

Until the 1970s, it was only possible to think of the individual being fulfilled in the context of the whole community. Religion is about dependence, on each other and on the world around us and all the stories of all religions are about how we manage that dependence and find in it strength and truth.

In the last three or four decades, with the rise of wealth and technology, a huge number of people can now believe that they are not dependent and that they are in control as individuals and this is historically completely new. So, the crisis we are approaching is completely new where the individual asks the question of whether it is possible to have a life which is not dependent on the rest of the community. A radically new question indeed!

And that is why the stories of our dependence – communism, socialism or European and American social democracy – are declining. This has happened because a critical mass of people believes that they are able to shape their own destiny. So, there isn't one story that works for everybody anymore. According to This is a frightening concept, especially for those who are dispossessed as they can ask the question, "Where is my story now?" The political stories have been taken from them and the only ones that remain are the religious ones and this is a phenomenon we are seeing from South America to Africa, from Asia to large parts of Europe (Kohli 2018). Our previous narrative was that everyone in the community had to be looked after by the welfare state. The rich and powerful do not share this story!

Therefore, the rich are taking a secular narrative of a collapsed social democratic system and turning it into a religious one. Such a story is bound to fail! Along with that, the story of the powerless will also! Urgently we need to figure out a shared story of love, compassion and joy!

> "We tell ourselves stories in order to live". For most of history, the value of the story was the extent to which it enabled us to understand our place in the big scheme of the world. "The difference between a story that was imagined and a story that was historical was not a central one; it was the effect of the story enabling us to live with each other"

70

You Will Never Be Famous

Despite all, we need to remain humble and realise that we are not meant to be great, powerful or famous persons. True humility and genuineness consist in accepting that we can be happy and fulfilled without being great. Without being the centre of attention of the whole world!

That is the title of an article in *New York Times*. It adds, "And that's OK." Its author, Emily Esfahani Smith, who also wrote *The Power of Meaning* (Smith 2017a), recommends that we spend time to George Eliot's "Middlemarch." (Smith 2017). Reading this book of 700-some pages, requires devotion and discipline, which is basically what we lack today! Understanding this book requires tremendous effort and commitment.

The heroine of this novel is Dorothea Brooke, a wealthy young gentlewoman in a provincial English town. Dorothea has a passionate temperament and yearns to accomplish some good in the world as a philanthropist. The novel's hero, Tertius Lydgate, is an ambitious young doctor who hopes to make important scientific discoveries. Both hope to lead great epic lives.

Both Dorothea and Tertius end up in disastrous marriages – she to the vicar Mr. Casaubon, he to the town beauty Rosamond. Slowly, their dreams wither away. Rosamond, who turns out to be vain and superficial, wants Tertius to pursue a career lucrative enough to support her indulgent tastes and by the end of the novel, he acquiesces, abandoning his scientific quest to become a doctor to the rich. Though conventionally "successful," he dies at 50 believing himself a failure for not following through on his original life plan (Smith 2017).

As for Dorothea, after the Reverend Casaubon dies, she marries her true love, Will Ladislaw. Her larger ambitions too go unrealized. She too has wasted her potential. Tertius's tragedy is that he never reconciles himself to his humdrum reality. Dorothea's triumph is that she does, notes Esfahani Smith (2017).

By novel's end, she settles into life as a wife and a mother and to use Eliot's terms the "foundress of nothing." It may be a disappointment for the reader, but not for Dorothea. She pours herself into her roles as mother and wife with "beneficent activity which she had not the doubtful pains of discovering and marking out for herself."

Looking out her window one day, Dorothea sees a family making its way down the road and realizes that she, too, is "a part of that involuntary, palpitating life and could neither look out on it from her luxurious shelter as a mere spectator, nor hide her eyes in selfish complaining." In other words, she begins to live in the moment. Rather than succumb to the despair of thwarted dreams, she embraces her life as it is and contributes to those around her as she can.

This is Eliot's final word on Dorothea: "Her full nature, like that river of which Cyrus broke the strength, spent itself in channels which had no great name on the earth. But the effect of her being on those around her was incalculably diffusive: for the growing good of the world is partly dependent on unhistorical acts; and that things are not so ill with you and me as they might have been is half owing to the number who lived faithfully a hidden life and rest in unvisited tombs."

This rich and profound passage encapsulates what a meaningful life is about: "connecting and contributing to something beyond the self, in whatever humble form that may take," according to Esfahani Smith (2017).

It has become each one's dream today to become great, to achieve something momentous and to change the world radically. Though they remain ideals, we should learn from Tertius's tragedy. Most of us, most of the time will live ordinary, mundane lives and will not become world-famous. That should never be the goal of our lives. It is to do the little and ordinary things with great love and devotion. Can we experience God in the small ordinary acts? These small caring acts make our lives wise and meaningful.

Most of us, most of the time will live ordinary, mundane lives and will not become world-famous. That should never be the goal of our lives. It is to do the little and ordinary things with great love and devotion. Can we experience God in the small ordinary acts? These small caring acts make our lives wise and meaningful.

Epilogue

Finding God in all Things and All Things in God. A painful, challenging and at the same time blissful process!

God is the "Wholly Other," (*ganz Andere*) the one who cannot be named or tamed. At the same time, the Bible speaks of God being present everyone. In our hearts and eyes. In the things of our life and everywhere: "Your Wisdom reaches mightily from one end of the earth to the other and she orders all things well" (Wis 8:1) and "Where can I go from your spirit? Or where can I flee from your presence? If I ascend to heaven, you are there; . . . If I take the wings of the morning and settle at the farthest limits of the sea, even there your hand shall lead me and your right hand shall hold me fast" (Ps 139:7-12). This speaks to the fact that God sustains the universe in existence from moment to moment, the way a singer sustains a song (Barron 2019).

The defining feature of the spirituality associated with St. Ignatius of Loyola; founder of the Jesuits is: "Finding God in all things." This flows from the Bible verse mentioned above. Despite his transcendence, God should not be thought of as distant in any conventional sense of the term, certainly not in the Deist manner. Rather, as Thomas Aquinas taught, God is in all things, "by essence, presence and power." In everything God is "personally and intentionally present, offering something of himself to us." So, the search for God can commence right here, right now, with whatever is at hand.

So, "Who is God?" or "Where is God?" The correct answer was "in everyone and everywhere." We may also add, in None or Nowhere. Once that truth sinks in, our lives irrevocably change, for now every person, every event, every sorrow, every encounter becomes an opportunity for communion with God. The 17th- century Jesuit spiritual master, Jean-Pierre de Caussade (2017), expressed the same idea when he said that everything that happens to us is, directly or indirectly, the will of God. Once again, it is impossible to accept the truth of that statement and remain the same person you were before. This always already graced quality of "all things" functions as the starting point for Ignatius's spirituality (Barron 2019).

Once we experience this truth that God is in everything, then the next step is quite easy and exceedingly difficult: to find everything in God. God and God alone is for us the source, origin, goal and end of our lives. This God is to be traced in the day to day things and activities of our life. If so these day to day activities and things become significant for us, since we experience them in God and in God alone. Thus every activity, experience and thing become important and significant for us, because in all of them, we see traces of God. All of them lead us to God. All of them invite us to experience God fully. Thus the things of this world are particularly important. At the same time, they are not absolutely important. Their worth, values and significance lie in God and in God alone.

Thus our life takes on a new fragrance and vitality since we can live in God. We can experience God in everyone and everything. And since everything leads us to God and God alone, we can truly experience the fullness of life also in our brokenness and frailties!

Bibliography

Adler, Felix. *Essentials of Spirituality*. [S.l.]: 2019. Outlook Verlag.

Adler, Warren. 2015. "Will Movies and TV Shows Eventually Kill the Written Word?" HuffPost Canada. September 25, 2015. https://www.huffingtonpost.com/warren-adler/will-movies-and-tv-shows-_b_8190580.html. If not explicitly mentioned, all internet sources assessed on May, 2019.

Adler, Warren. 2015a. *Torture Man: A Novel.* New York: Rosetta Press.

Allen Jr, John L. 2016. "Pope Francis Practices the Politics of Memory in Armenia." *Crux* (blog). June 26, 2016. https://cruxnow.com/francis-in-armenia/2016/06/25/pope-francis-politics-memory/.

"An Economist Has Studied the Data and Concluded God Exists." 2017, May 17. The Independent. http://www.independent.co.uk/life-style/existence-of-god-rational-arguments-mathematics-human-consciousness-a7739841.html.

Anuradha. n.d. "Brahma Creates the Universe - All About Hinduism." Accessed August 6, 2019. http://www.allabouthinduism.info/2013/03/06/brahma-creates/.

Arizona State University. 2019, Apr 15. "The history of humanity in your face." ScienceDaily. <www.sciencedaily.com/releases/2019/04/190415113813.htm>.

Association for Psychological Science. 2016, Apr 8. "Curiosity leads us to seek out unpleasant, painful outcomes." ScienceDaily. <www.sciencedaily. com/releases/2016/04 /160408101933.htm>.

Barron, Robert Bishop. 2019, July 23. "Finding God in All Things." *Word on Fire*. https://www.wordonfire.org/resources/article/finding-god-in-all-things/24633/.

Basu, Indrani. 2015. "These Stories We Covered In 2015 Highlight All That Is Right With The World." HuffPost India. December 31, 2015. https://www.huffingtonpost.in/2015/12/31/2015-heartwarming-stories_n_8892830.html.

Becker, Ernest. 2009. *The Denial of Death*. Ashland, Or.

Begum, Tahmina. 2018. "'I'm Happy, But I Could Be Happier': How Love Island Reflects Our Throwaway Dating Culture." HuffPost UK. July 27, 2018. https://www.huffingtonpost.co.uk/entry/im-happy-but-i-could-be-happier-the-danger-of-eternally-swiping-right_uk_5b51ec6be4b0fd5c73c4a458.

Benson, Robert Hugh and Simon Vance. 2017. *Lord of the World*. Ashland, Oregon]: Blackstone Audio.

Berdyaev, Nikolai. 1932. "Spiritual Condition of the Contemporary World." http://www.berdyaev.com/berdiaev/berd_lib/1932_377.html.

Berdyaev, Nikolai. 1939. "The Paradox of the Lie." Accessed June 2, 2019. http://www.berdyaev.com/berdiaev/berd_lib/1939_xxx.html.

Beres, Derek. 2017. "Being Busy Is Killing Our Ability to Think Creatively." Big Think. July 3, 2017. https://bigthink.com/21st-century-spirituality/creativity-and-distraction.

Beres, Derek. 2017a "How Reading Rewires Your Brain for Greater Intelligence and Empathy." Big Think. 2017a-09-11T20:22:12+00:00. https://bigthink.com/21st-century-spirituality/reading-rewires-your-brain-for-more-intelligence-and-empathy.

Beres, Derek. 2017. *Whole Motion: Training Your Brain and Body for Optimal Health.*

Berger, Rabbi. 1986. "Rabbi Berger: 'Can You Imagine Knowing That in a Few Moments Death Was Imminent?', Five Minutes to Live, Yom Kippur - 1986." Speakola. 1986. https://speakola.com/ideas/rabbi-berger-five-minutes-to-live-yom-kippur-1986.

Bergland, Christopher. 2018. "Empathic People Use Social Brain Circuitry to Process Music." Psychology Today. June 18, 2018. https://www.psychologytoday.com/blog/the-athletes-way/201806/empathic-people-use-social-brain-circuitry-process-music.

Blumberg, Antonia. 2017. "Morgan Freeman Explores What Unites The World's Religions In 'The Story Of God.'" *HuffPost India*. January 14, 2017. https://www.huffpost.com/entry/morgan-freeman-explores-what-unites-the-worlds-religions-in-the-story-of-god_n_58791661e4b09281d0eaa0f0.

Bradberry, Travis. 2019. "Why You Should Spend Your Money On Experiences, Not Things." Forbes. 2019. https://www.forbes.com/sites/travisbradberry/2016/08/09/why-you-should-spend-your-money-on-experiences-not-things/.

Bradberry, Travis. 2009. *Emotional Intelligence 2.0*. San Diego, CA : TalentSmart.

Briggs, Jean L. 1981. *Never in Anger*. Harvard University Press.

Brigham Young University. 2017. "How Eating Less Can Slow the Aging Process." *ScienceDaily*. February 13, 2017. https://www.sciencedaily.com/releases/2017/02/170213151306.htm.

"Calvin and Hobbes – Art Before Commerce." 2016, May 23. https://www.buttondown.tv/creative/calvin-hobbes-art-commerce/.

Carey, Benedict. 2019. "Johns Hopkins Opens New Center for Psychedelic Research." *The New York Times*, September 4, 2019, sec. Science. https://www.nytimes.com/2019/09/04/science/psychedelic-drugs-hopkins-depression.html.

Cell Press. 2018. "Viruses influenced gene sharing between Neanderthals and humans." ScienceDaily, 4 October 2018. <www.sciencedaily.com/releases/ 2018/10/181004112547.htm>.

Chiorando, Maria. 2019, June 4. "Vegan Climate Activist Greta Thunberg On Cover Of 'WIRED' Magazine." June 4. https://www.plantbasednews.org/post/vegan-climate-greta-thunberg-cover-wired-magazine.

Coventry University. 2018, Feb 5. "Meditation has limited role in making you a better person, says study" *ScienceDaily*. <www.sciencedaily.com/releases/2018/02/180205092902.htm>.

Caussade, Jean Pierre de, and J. Ramière. 2017. *Abandonment to Divine Providence*. North Palm Beach, Florida : Beacon Publishing.

David Scott. 2013. "Mother Teresa's Long Dark Night." chapter 17 in *The Love That Made Mother Teresa*. Manchester, NH: Sophia Institute Press, 107-113.

David, Susan A. 2016. *Emotional Agility: Get Unstuck, Embrace Change, and Thrive in Work and Life*.

Deterline, Brooke. 2017. "The Power of Forgiveness at Work - Thrive Global." October 2, 2017. https://thriveglobal.com/stories/the-power-of-forgiveness-at-work/.

Devdutt, Patnaik. 2017. "How Did the World Come into Being According to Hinduism?" September 2017. https://www.dailyo.in/variety/hindusim-world-creation-universe-brahma-vishu-shiva/story/1/19522.html.

Dixit, Shubhra. 2016. "'Art before Commerce': A Video Essay on 'Calvin and Hobbes' and What Made the Comic Strip so Special." Text. *Scroll.in*. May 25, 2016. https://scroll.in/video/808677/art-before-commerce-a-video-essay-on-calvin-and-hobbes-and-what-made-the-comic-strip-so-special.

Donbishopsam. 2016. "How We Learned to Stop Worrying About People and Love the Bombing." Club de Mediapart. January 11, 2016. https://blogs.mediapart.fr/donbishopsam/blog/110116/how-we-learned-stop-worrying-about-people-and-love-bombing.

Doucleff, Michaeleen, and Jane Greenhalgh. 2019. "How Inuit Parents Teach Kids to Control Their Anger." MPR News. 2019. https://www.mprnews.org/story/2019/03/13/npr-a-playful-way-to-teach-kids-to-control-their-anger.

Drexel University. 2017. "Brain imaging headband measures how our minds align when we communicate." ScienceDaily. 27 February 2017. <www.sciencedaily.com/releases/2017/02/170227082207.htm>.

Duke University. 2016. "Oxytocin Enhances Spirituality, New Study Says." September 21, 2016. https://medicalxpress.com/news/2016-09-oxytocin-spirituality.html.

Editors. 2017. "How to Break Free from the Tyranny of Positivity | Heleo." Next Big Idea Club. February 8, 2017. https://heleo.com/conversation-embrace-authenticity-how-to-break-free-from-the-tyranny-of-positivity/12784/.

Faleiro, Sonia. 2017. "Opinion | Why Do So Many Indian Children Go Missing?" *The New York Times*, November 19, 2017, sec. Opinion. https://www.nytimes.com/2017/11/19/opinion/missing-children-india.html.

Faleiro, Sonia. 2012. *Beautiful Thing: Inside the Secret World of Bombay's Dance Bars.* New York: Black Cat.

Field Museum. 2019, Apr 18. "The secret to a stable society? A steady supply of beer doesn't hurt: Archaeologists recreate ancient brewing techniques to learn how beer kept an empire afloat." ScienceDaily. <www.sciencedaily.com/releases/2019/04/190418080814.htm>.

Fisher, Richard. n.d. "The Perils of Short-Termism: Civilisation's Greatest Threat." Accessed June 6, 2019. http://www.bbc.com/future/story/20190109-the-perils-of-short-termism-civilisations-greatest-threat.

Fuller, Robert C. 2010. *Spiritual, But Not Religious: Understanding Unchurched America.* Oxford: Oxford Univ. Press.

Francis, Pope. 2015. *Laudato Si': On Care for Our Common Home.* Huntington: Our Sunday Visitor.

Gawande, Atul. 2017. *Being Mortal: Medicine and What Matters in the End.* New York : Picador, Metropolitan Books, Henry Holt & Company.

Green, Emma. 2016. "Pope Francis and Mark Zuckerberg Meet at the Vatican, Perhaps Intending to Break the Internet." The Atlantic. August 29, 2016. https://www.theatlantic.com/technology/archive/2016/08/pope-francis-meets-with-mark-zuckberg/497819/.

Greene, Alanda. 2017. "Singing to Tomatoes." *Daily Good.* February 7, 2017. http://www.dailygood.org/story/1507/singing-to-tomatoes/.

Goldstein, Barry. 2016. "4 Surprising Ways That Music Changes Your Brain and Influences Your Mood." May 9, 2016. https://www.consciouslifestylemag.com/music-and-the-brain-affects-mood/.

Gregoire, Carolyn. 2016, Mar 5. "Why Silence Is So Good for Your Brain." HuffPost. 00:23 500. https://www.huffpost.com/entry/silence-brain-benefits_n_56d83967e4b0000de4037004.

Guardini, Romano. *The End of the Modern World.* Wilmington, Delaware : ISI Books, 1998.

Harris, Elise. 2019. "Top Vatican Official Echoes Müller, Says Dialogue Key to Political Disagreement." *Crux* (blog). May 30, 2019. https://cruxnow.com/vatican/2019/05/30/top-vatican-official-echoes-muller-says-dialogue-key-to-political-disagreement/.

Harris, Michael. 2015. *The End of Absence: Reclaiming What We've Lost in a World of Constant Connection.*

Hawking, S.W. 2016. *A Brief History of Time: From the Big Bang to Black Holes.* London: Bantam Books.

Hawking, Stephen W., and Leonard Mlodinow. 2010. *The Grand Design.* New York: Bantam.

Heaven, Douglas. n.d. "The Uncertain Future of Democracy." Accessed June 6, 2019. http://www.bbc.com/future/story/20170330-the-uncertain-future-of-democracy.

Hill, Nancy. 2016. "Three Things That Matter Most in Youth and Old Age by Nancy Hill — YES! Magazine." *Yes! Magazine.* July 18, 2016. https://www.yesmagazine.org/happiness/three-things-that-matter-most-in-youth-and-old-age-20160718.

Hoffer, Eric. 2002. *The True Believer*. New York: Perennial.

Hook, Leslie. 2017. "Artificial Intelligence: Silicon Valley's New Deity." Financial Times. October 25, 2017. https://www.ft.com/content/4c89d6cc-b90c-11e7-9bfb-4a9c83ffa852.

House, Freeman. 2000. *Totem Salmon: Life Lessons from Another Species*. New York: Beacon Press, 2000.

Huckabee, Tyler. 2017, May 16. "What Bill Nye and the science movement can learn from religion," *The Washington Post*.

IAU1812. 2018. "International Astronomical Union | IAU." October 28, 2018. https://www.iau.org/news/pressreleases/detail/iau1812/.

James, William. 2019. *The Varieties of Religious Experience*. New York: Nova Science Publishers, Incorporated.

Jamison, Christopher. 2008. *Finding Happiness: Monastic Steps for a Fulfilling Life*. London: Orion Audiobooks.

Kaufman, Sarah L. et al. 2017, Sept 18. "This is your brain on art" *The Washington Post*.

Karimundackal, Thomas and Kuruvilla Pandikattu (eds). 2019. *Logic and Love: Reflecting on Professor John Vattanky's Contribution to Indian Philosophy and Spirituality*, New Delhi: Christian World Imprints.

Kentish, Benjamin. 2016. "Religious People Understand the World Less, Study Finds." The Independent. October 25, 2016. http://www.independent.co.uk/news/science/religious-people-understand-world-less-study-shows-a7378896.html.

Khaira, Rachna. 2019. "Meet Christo Thomas, The Architect Behind UN's International Day Of Education." HuffPost India. January 26, 2019. https://www.huffingtonpost.in/entry/meet-christo-thomas-indian-architect-of-un-international-day-of-education_in_5c4c229fe4b06ba6d3bd4aa3.

Kohli, Diya. 2018. "Science Explains and Religion Gives Meaning to the World: Neil MacGregor." Https://Www.Livemint.Com. November 25, 2018. https://www.livemint.com/Companies/fRzSi2L89cfzwEZgW9HjYL/Science-explains-and-religion-gives-meaning-to-the-world-Ne.html.

Krista, Trippett. 2017. "Atul Gawande — What Matters in the End." The On Being Project. October 26, 2017. https://onbeing.org/programs/atul-gawande-what-matters-in-the-end/.

Krznaric, Roman. n.d. "Why We Need to Reinvent Democracy for the Long-Term." Accessed June 7, 2019. http://www.bbc.com/future/story/20190318-can-we-reinvent-democracy-for-the-long-term.

Kuhn, Gustav. 2019. "Mind Games: What Magic Reveals about How Our Brains Work." *The Guardian*, March 30, 2019, sec. Life and style. https://www.theguardian.com/lifeandstyle/2019/mar/30/mind-games-what-magic-reveals-about-how-our-brains-work.

Kuhn, Gustav. 2019. *Experiencing the Impossible: The Science of Magic*. Cambridge : MIT Press.

Kumar, Rohit. 2016. "This May Help You Make Sense Of Donald Trump's Popularity."

HuffPost India. May 19, 2016. https://www.huffingtonpost.in/rohit-kumar/this-may-help-you-make-sense-of-donald-trumps-popularity_a_21418958/.

Lawton, Graham, and Jeremy Webb. 2019. *How to Be Human*. London: John Murray.

Levitan, Corey. 2017. "How SIO's Dr. Ram Talks Science to Religious Leaders." *La Jolla Light*. November 29, 2017. https://www.lajollalight.com/lifestyle/sd-cm-ljl-science-to-religious-20171129-story.html.

Levitin, Daniel J., and Luke Daniels. 2015. *The Organized Mind: Thinking Straight in the Age of Information Overload*. 2015.

Lindley, Robin. 2017, Dec 6. "How Our Stone-Age Brain Undermines Smart Politics: An Interview with Rick Shenkman." *HuffPost*. https://www.huffpost.com/entry/how-our-stone-age-brain-u_b_10109356.

Livni, Ephrat. 2018. "Scientists Found the Spiritual Part of Our Brains—Religion Not Required." Quartz. May 30, 2018. https://qz.com/1292368/columbia-and-yale-scientists-just-found-the-spiritual-part-of-our-brains/.

Lowman, Meg. 2017. "Of Science And Religion - Can Spiritual Values Of Forests Inspire Conservation?" HuffPost. May 24, 2017. https://www.huffpost.com/entry/of-science-and-religion-can-spiritual-values-of-forests_b_5925d6cfe4b0aa7207986a39.

Macgregor, Neil. 2019. *Living with the Gods: On Beliefs and Peoples*. New York: Vintage Books.

Macy, Joanna. 2017. "The Greatest Danger." Daily Good. December 9, 2017. http://www.dailygood.org/story/1821/the-greatest-danger/.

Martín, Inés San. 2016. "Pope Francis Tells Europe, 'I Have a Dream.'" *Crux* (blog). May 6, 2016. https://cruxnow.com/church/2016/05/06/pope-francis-tells-europe-i-have-a-dream/.

Max-Planck-Gesellschaft. 2017. "Epigenetics between the generations: We inherit more than just genes." *ScienceDaily*. 17 July 2017. <www.sciencedaily.com/releases/2017/07/170717100548.htm>.

Maye, Brian. 2018. "Fr Georges Lemaître: An Irishman's Diary about the Father of the Big Bang." The Irish Times. July 17, 2018. https://www.irishtimes.com/opinion/fr-georges-lema%C3%AEtre-an-irishman-s-diary-about-the-father-of-the-big-bang-1.2689491.

McGall, Daniel. 2017, Mar 12."Science and Religion Must Go Together" *The Augustha Chronicle*.

Michaelis, Ben. 2013. *Your Next Big Thing: 10 Small Steps to Get Moving and Get Happy*. New York: Wolf Street Press.

Mooney, Chris, and Brady Dennis. 2018. "The World Has Just over a Decade to Get Climate Change under Control, U.N. Scientists Say." *The Washington Post*, October 7, 2018, sec. Energy and Environment. https://www.washingtonpost.com/energy-environment/2018/10/08/world-has-only-years-get-climate-change-under-control-un-scientists-say/.

Morris, Steven. 2019. "Woodland Sounds Help Relaxation More than Meditation Apps - Study." *The Guardian*, September 12, 2019, sec. UK news. https://www.theguardian.com/uk-news/2019/sep/13/woodland-sounds-help-relaxation-more-than-meditation-apps-study.

Mulligan, Jesse. 2017. "What Does It Mean to Be Human?" *RNZ*. November 27, 2017. https://www.rnz.co.nz/national/programmes/afternoons/audio/2018623200/what-does-it-mean-to-be-human.

Muralidharan, Kavitha. 2019. "When Two Poets from Jharkhand And Kashmir Met in Chennai." HuffPost India. January 19, 2019. https://www.huffingtonpost.in/entry/jacinta-kerketta-nighat-sahiba-kashmir-jharkhand-poems-language_in_5c41f480e4b027c3bbc14a3a.

Nelson, Robert H. 2017. "An Economist Has Studied the Data and Concluded God Exists." *The Independent*. May 17, 2017. http://www.independent.co.uk/life-style/existence-of-god-rational-arguments-mathematics-human-consciousness-a7739841.html.

Nelson, Robert H. 2016. *God? Very Probably: Five Rational Ways to Think About the Question of God.*

Newport, Cal. 2018. *Deep Work: Rules for Focused Success in a Distracted World.* Baltimore: Grand Central Pub.

Nicholson, Paul. 2008. "Finding Happiness: Monastic Steps for a Fulfilling Life." Thinking Faith: The Online Journal of the Jesuits in Britain. October 14, 2008. https://www.thinkingfaith.org/articles/book_20081014_1.htm.

Nick, Watts. 2011. "The King and the Maiden By Søren Kierkegaard | Reading Theology." *Reading Theology*. 2011. https://www.readingtheology.com/the-king-and-the-maiden-by-s%C3%B8ren-kierkegaard.

Nuwer, Rachel. 2018. "What If We Knew When and How We'd Die?" June 18, 2018. https://www.bbc.com/future/article/20180618-what-if-we-knew-when-we-were-going-to-die.

Pandikattu, Kuruvilla and PT Mathew (eds). 2019. *Committed to the Church and the Country: Exploring the Theological Contributions of Prof. Dr Kurien Kunnumpuram SJ,* New Delhi: Christian World Imprints.

Pandikattu, Kuruvilla, and Thomas Karimundackal (eds). 2018. *Melodies from the Flute, Dialogue Among Religions and Cultures: Memorial Volume for Indian Christian Philosopher Rev. Noel Sheth SJ.* Pune: Jnana Deepa (JD).

Pascal, Blaise. 1972. *Pensées*. Paris: Librairie Generale Francaise.

Patrick, Stewart. 2014. "A Man-Made Ecological Catastrophe: More Than Half of All Earth's Vertebrates Have Disappeared." Text. *The National Interest*. October 10, 2014. https://nationalinterest.org/blog/the-buzz/man-made-ecological-catastrophe-more-half-all-earth%E2%80%99s-11446.

Pembroke, Ella Saltmarshe and Beatrice. n.d. "How Art and Culture Can Help Us Rethink Time." Accessed June 7, 2019. http://www.bbc.com/future/story/20190521-how-art-and-culture-can-help-us-rethink-time.

Philip, Pullella. 2015. "Media Should Give More Space to Good News, Pope Says after Grim Year." *Reuters*, December 31, 2015. https://www.reuters.com/article/us-pope-media-idUSKBN0UE16P20151231.

"Pope Ends First Day of Holy Land Visit with Message of Unity, Brotherhood | *The Times of Israel*." n.d. Accessed May 3, 2019. https://www.timesofisrael.com/pope-francis-to-touch-down-in-bethlehem-sunday-morning/.

Popova, Maria. 2019. "Lorraine Hansberry on Depression and Its Most Reliable Antidote." *Brain Pickings* (blog). October 7, 2019. https://www.brainpickings.org/2019/10/07/lorraine-hansberry-depression/.

Popova, Maria. 2018. "Loneliness in Time: Physicist Freeman Dyson on Immigration and How Severing Our Connection to the Past Shallows Our Present and Hollows Our History." *Brain Pickings* (blog). August 8, 2018. https://www.brainpickings.org/2018/08/08/freeman-dyson-immigration/.

Popova, Maria. 2017. "The Courage to Be Yourself: E.E. Cummings on Art, Life, and Being Unafraid to Feel." *Brain Pickings* (blog). September 25, 2017. https://www.brainpickings.org/2017/09/25/e-e-cummings-advice/.

Purcell, Conor. 2018. "Carlo Rovelli on Schrödinger, God and Physics Being 'Better than LSD.'" The Irish Times. April 9, 2018. https://www.irishtimes.com/news/science/carlo-rovelli-on-schr%C3%B6dinger-god-and-physics-being-better-than-lsd-1.3455527.

Purser, Ronald. 2019. "The Mindfulness Conspiracy." *The Guardian*, June 14, 2019, sec. Life and style. https://www.theguardian.com/lifeandstyle/2019/jun/14/the-mindfulness-conspiracy-capitalist-spirituality.

Ratner, Paul. 2016. "Study: Religious and Superstitious People Struggle to Understand the Physical World." *Big Think*. October 28, 2016. https://bigthink.com/paul-ratner/study-religious-people-struggle-to-understand-the-physical-world.

Rice-Oxley, Jon Henley Mark. 2019. "Europe 'Coming Apart before Our Eyes', Say 30 Top Intellectuals." *The Guardian*, January 25, 2019, sec. World news. https://www.theguardian.com/world/2019/jan/25/europe-coming-apart-before-our-eyes-say-30-top-intellectuals.

Robert, Kaplan. n.d. "What Is the Origin of Zero? How Did We Indicate Nothingness before Zero?" *Scientific American*. Accessed August 6, 2019. https://www.scientificamerican.com/article/what-is-the-origin-of-zer/.

Rolf, Veronica Mary. 2019. "'Alle Shalle Be Wele.' Julian of Norwich and the Process of Transformation." *OpenDemocracy*. February 10, 2019. https://www.opendemocracy.net/en/transformation/alle-shalle-be-wele-julian-of-norwich-and-process-of-transformatio/.

Rovelli, Carlo. 2019. *Order of Time*. New York: Penguin Books.

Royce, Josiah. 1998. *The Works of Josiah Royce: The Philosophy of Loyalty*. Charlottesville, Va: InteLex Corporation.

Rubin, Charles T. 2019. "Eclipse of Man." *The New Atlantis*. 2019. https://www.thenewatlantis.com/publications/eclipse-of-man.

Rubin, Charles T. 2014. *Eclipse of Man: Human Extinction and the Meaning of Progress*. New York: Encounter Books.

Salyer, Jerry. 2015. "To Be, Or Not To Be (Human)." March 17, 2015. https://www.catholicworldreport.com/2015/03/17/to-be-or-not-to-be-human/.

Schmidt, Leigh Eric.2012. *Restless Souls: The Making of American Spirituality*. Berkeley, Calif: University of California Press.

Scott, David. 2013. "Mother Teresa's Long Dark Night." *Catholic Education Research Centre*. 2013. https://www.catholiceducation.org/en/faith-and-character/faith-and-character/mother-teresas-long-dark-night.html.

Shenkman, Richard. 2016. *Political Animals: How Our Stone-Age Brain Gets in the Way of Smart Politics*

Sheth, Noel. 1984. *The Divinity of Krishna*. New Delhi: Munshiram Manoharlal.

Smith, Emily Esfahani. 2017. "Opinion | You'll Never Be Famous — And That's O.K." *The New York Times*, September 4, 2017, sec. Opinion. https://www.nytimes.com/2017/09/04/opinion/middlemarch-college-fame.html.

Smith, Emily Esfahani. 2017a. *The Power of Meaning: Crafting a Life That Matters*. Toronto : Viking, 2017.

Society for Personality and Social Psychology. 2017, Jan 21. "Facts, beliefs, and identity: The seeds of science skepticism." *ScienceDaily*,. <www.sciencedaily .com/releases/2017 /01/170121183252.htm>.

Specktor, Brandon. 2018. "Stephen Hawking's Final Book Says There's 'No Possibility' of God in Our Universe." *Live Science*. October 17, 2018. https://www.livescience.com/63854-stephen-hawking-says-no-god.html.

Spitzer Robert J. 2015. *The Soul's Upward Yearning: Clues to Our Transcendent Nature from Experience and Reason*. San Francisco: Ignatius Press.

Stefan, Stenudd. n.d. "The Paradox of Origin - The Creation in Rig Veda 10:129." *Creation Myths*. Accessed August 6, 2019. https://www.creationmyths.org/rigveda-10-129-indian-creation/.

Suchocki, Marjorie. 1991. "Original Sin Revisited." *Religion Online* (blog). 1991. https://www.religion-online.org/article/original-sin-revisited/.

Tegmark, Max. 2015. *Our Mathematical Universe: My Quest for the Ultimate Nature of Reality*.

Teresa, Mother and Brian Kolodiejchuk. *Mother Teresa: Come Be My Light: the Private Writings of the "Saint of Calcutta"*. Bangalore: Asian Trading Corporation, 2014.

"The Bard's Anniversary." 2016. The Irish Times. April 23, 2016. https://www.irishtimes.com/opinion/editorial/the-bard-s-anniversary-1.2620656.

The Editors. n.d. "Sunyata | Buddhist Concept." *Encyclopedia Britannica*. Accessed August 6, 2019. https://www.britannica.com/topic/sunyata.

Tick, Edward. 2012. *War and the Soul: Healing Our Nation's Veterans from Post-Tramatic Stress Disorder*. Wheaton: Quest Books.

TNN. 2015. "'Operation Sulaimani': Aim to Feed Needy in Kozhikode Hotels | Kozhikode News - Times of India." *The Times of India*. June 15, 2015. https://timesofindia.indiatimes.

com/city/kozhikode/Operation-Sulaimani-Aim-to-feed-needy-in-Kozhikode-hotels/articleshow/47684573.cms.

Tolle, Eckhart. 2018. *The Power of Now: A Guide to Spiritual Enlightenment.* Sydney, NSW: Hachette Australia.

United Nations. 2009. "Indian Teenager Seeks Urgent Action from Leaders on Climate Change." *Deccan Herald.* September 23, 2009. https://www.deccanherald.com/content/26857/indian-teenager-seeks-urgent-action.html.

University of Missouri. 2015. "Negative Spiritual Beliefs Associated with More Pain and Worse Physical, Mental Health." *Technology Org* (blog). September 24, 2015. https://www.technology.org/2015/09/24/negative-spiritual-beliefs-associated-pain-worse-physical-mental-health/.

University of Texas at Austin. 2019, Mar 22. "To stoke creativity, crank out ideas and then step away." *ScienceDaily.* <www.sciencedaily.com/releases/2019/03/190322093856.htm>.

University of California - San Francisco. 2019, June 3. "Meditation goes digital in new clinical trial: Individualized program improves attention and memory in healthy young adults." *ScienceDaily.* <www.sciencedaily.com/releases/2019/06/190603124705.htm>.

University of Toronto, Rotman School of Management. 2019, Apr 4."To keep the creative juices flowing, employees should be receptive to criticism." *ScienceDaily.* <www.sciencedaily.com/releases/2019/04/190404132534.htm>.

VanDenBerghe, Betsy. 2016. "Spiritual IQ in a Secular Age | RealClearReligion." April 28, 2016. https://www.realclearreligion.org/articles/2016/04/29/spiritual_iq_in_a_secular_age_107116.html."Visit of the Holy Father to Israel and Palestine - Google Search." n.d. Accessed May 3, 2019. https://www.google.com/search?client=firefox-b-1-d&q=visit+of+the+Holy+Father+to+Israel+and+Palestine.

Wake Forest Baptist Medical Center. 2019, Aug 15. "Adults with mild cognitive impairment can learn and benefit from mindfulness meditation." *ScienceDaily.* <www.sciencedaily.com/releases/2019/08/190815140852.htm>.

Walters, Kerry. 2016. "Mother Teresa: A Saint Who Conquered Darkness." *Franciscan Spirit.* 2016. https://blog.franciscanmedia.org/franciscan-spirit/mother-teresa-a-saint-who-conquered-darkness.

Walters, Kerry S. 2016a. *St. Teresa of Calcutta: Missionary, Mother, Mystic.* Cincinnati: Franciscan Media.

Walton, Alice G. 2017. "The Science of Spirituality: A Psychologist And A Neuroscientist Explain Being 'In The Flow.'" *Forbes.* 2017. https://www.forbes.com/sites/alicegwalton/2017/08/22/the-science-of-spirituality-a-psychologist-and-a-neuroscientist-explain-being-in-the-flow/.

Weller, Francis. 2019. "Drinking the Tears of the World: Grief as Deep Activism, By Francis Weller | *Carolyn Baker.*" February 3, 2019. https://carolynbaker.net/2019/03/15/drinking-the-tears-of-the-world-grief-as-deep-activism-by-francis-weller/.

Wilson, Edward O. 2017. *Half-Earth: Our Planet's Fight for Life*. New York: Liveright Publishing Corporation.

Wolf, Richard. 2018, June 7. "'Beware the Robots:' Chief Justice John Roberts' Commencement Warning." *USA Today*. http://www.usatoday.com/story/news/politics/2018/06/07/beware-robots-chief-justice-john-roberts-commencement-warning/681626002/.

Yip. 2016. "People Who Trust Technology Are Happier." *Greater Good*. October 20, 2016. https://greatergood.berkeley.edu/article/item/people_who_trust_technology_are_happier.

Zausmer, Julie. 2017, Feb 27. "A Scientist's New Theory: Religion Was Key to Human's Social Evolution." *The Washington Post*.

www.ingramcontent.com/pod-product-compliance
Ingram Content Group UK Ltd.
Pitfield, Milton Keynes, MK11 3LW, UK
UKHW041857190726
13854UKWH00002B/946